All-New Healthy Soul Food Recipes

Publications International, Ltd.

American Heart Association® | American Stroke Association®
Learn and Live℠

CONTENTS

© 2007 Publications International, Ltd.

Recipes and text © 2007 American Heart Association.

All rights reserved. This publication may not be reproduced or quoted in whole or in part by any means whatsoever without written permission from:

Louis Weber, CEO
Publications International, Ltd.
7373 North Cicero Avenue
Lincolnwood, IL 60712

Permission is never granted for commercial purposes.

American Heart Association Team: Linda Ball, Deborah Renza, Janice Moss, Jackie Haigney, Robin Sullivan, Barthy Gaitonde, and Michelle Overcash

Recipe Developers: Maurietta Amos, Jennifer Booker, Nancy S. Hughes, Annie King, Carol Ritchie, and Julie Shapero, RD, LD

Recipe Analyst: Tammi Hancock, RD

Pictured on the front cover: Crab Cakes *(page 28)*.

Pictured on the back cover: *(clockwise from top):* Hot-Wing-Flavored Chicken with Ranch Sauce *(page 38)*, Orange Pound Cake with Mixed Berries *(page 82)*, and Zesty Three-Bean Salad *(page 14)*.

ISBN-13: 978-1-4127-2945-1
ISBN-10: 1-4127-2945-9

Manufactured in China.

8 7 6 5 4 3 2 1

Microwave Cooking: Microwave ovens vary in wattage. Use the cooking times as guidelines and check for doneness before adding more time.

Donations to the American Heart Association support its lifesaving work. For more information, call 1-800-AHA-USA1 (1-800-242-8721), contact us at americanheart.org, or write us at 7272 Greenville Avenue, Dallas, TX 75231.

For Publications International, Ltd., business inquiries call 847-329-5841; for consumer inquiries call 847-329-5657.

RECIPES

American Heart Association® | American Stroke Association®

POWER TO END STROKE℠
You are the Power

Power To End Stroke is an education and awareness campaign that embraces and celebrates the culture, energy, creativity, and lifestyles of African Americans. The American Stroke Association, a division of the American Heart Association, invites you to join us in reducing the incidence of stroke in our communities.

Cardiovascular disease, including stroke, causes about 30 percent of all deaths among African American men and 40 percent among women. In a recent survey, the American Stroke Association found that although 70 percent of African American adults felt they were knowledgeable about stroke, only 30 percent knew how to define it correctly. Blacks are almost twice as likely as whites to have a first stroke, yet only about 50 percent of the respondents knew the symptoms.

You can help improve these numbers. Join the movement and feel the power:

Put down the cigarettes and stop smoking.

Observe advice from your doctor and know your family's medical history.

Watch your weight and be physically active at least 30 minutes most days of the week.

Eat healthfully and avoid foods high in saturated fat, trans fat, cholesterol, and sodium.

Regulate and control high blood pressure, high blood cholesterol, and diabetes.

GO FOR THE GOAL

You have the power to fight stroke—and win! Take these steps to make a personal commitment to end stroke.

■ **Take the pledge and learn the warning signs.** Make your own statement to not just survive, but thrive! See page 25 for details on taking the pledge and information about the warning signs of stroke.

■ **Be proud and pass it on.** Once you've joined, you can help advance the cause by spreading the word to your family and friends. Make sure the people around you learn to recognize a stroke and act quickly. Send a list of the warning signs today to someone you care about.

■ **Involve your place of worship.** Our places of worship are the heart of our community, not only providing spiritual comfort but also serving as the support center for social, educational, and health issues.

■ **Volunteer your time or financial support.** The American Stroke Association has many ways for you to help fight against stroke and offers programs and events nationwide. Visit **local.StrokeAssociation.org** to find out what's happening near you.

■ **Shop Power.** Support the Power To End Stroke movement by visiting our online store at **shoppower.org**. Every purchase contributes to the fight against stroke in African Americans.

For more information on the American Stroke Association or how you can join the movement to fight stroke, call **1-888-4-STROKE** or visit **StrokeAssociation.org/power**.

Follow the three "Rs" to help protect yourself against stroke.

- **Reduce** your chances of having a stroke by learning the risk factors and working with your doctor.

- **Recognize** the warning signs of stroke. Stroke is a medical emergency—every second counts!

- **Respond** by calling 9-1-1 immediately if you or someone nearby is experiencing the warning signs of stroke. Then check the time that the first symptoms started. You'll need this information later.

Recipes

You use your power every day by choosing what to eat and how to live your life. The choices you make add up to a big impact on your overall health. When you make good choices, you and your family will enjoy the benefits for years to come. The important thing is to be physically active and develop healthy eating habits. That means eating a wide variety of foods that promote good health.

Whether you are eating at home or dining out, use your power wisely and follow the recommendations below to help protect your heart:

■ Eat a variety of nutritious foods from all food groups.

- Eat a diet rich in vegetables and fruits.

- Choose whole-grain, high-fiber foods.

- Eat fish, preferably oily fish, at least twice a week.

■ Limit foods that are high in calories but low in nutrients.

- Limit how much saturated fat, trans fat, and cholesterol you eat.

- Choose fat-free and low-fat dairy products.

- Cut back on beverages and foods with added sugars.

- Choose and prepare foods with little or no salt.

- If you drink alcohol, drink in moderation.

■ Read nutrition facts labels and ingredients lists when you shop.

For more information on the updated American Heart Association Dietary and Lifestyle Recommendations, visit **americanheart.org**.

How to Use These Recipes

To help you with meal planning, each recipe includes a nutrition analysis. The following guidelines give some details about how the analyses are calculated. Use the analyses to help determine how well a certain dish will fit into your overall eating plan.

■ Each analysis is for a single serving; garnishes or optional ingredients are not included.

■ When ingredient options are listed, the first one is analyzed. When a range of ingredients is given, the average is analyzed.

■ Values for saturated, monounsaturated, and polyunsaturated fats are rounded and may not add up to the amount listed for total fat. Total fat also includes other fatty substances and glycerol.

■ Processed foods can be very high in sodium. To keep levels of sodium in our recipes low, we use unprocessed foods or low-sodium products when possible, and we add table salt sparingly for flavor. This way you control the amount of salt you add. If you use the amounts specified, your use will not raise the sodium level as much as if you used a food processed with salt.

■ The reduced-fat cheese we use for analysis has no more than 6 grams of fat per ounce.

■ When meat, poultry, or seafood is marinated and the marinade is discarded, we calculate only the amount of marinade absorbed.

■ Meat statistics are based on cooked lean meat with all visible fat discarded.

■ We use 95% fat-free ground beef for analysis.

■ We use the abbreviations "g" for gram and "mg" for milligram.

Soups

CHICKEN SOUP WITH MUSTARD GREENS AND TOMATOES

SERVES 4 ▇ *1 cup per serving*

- 4 cups fat-free, low-sodium chicken broth
- 1 small carrot, thinly sliced
- 4 large mustard green leaves, coarsely chopped (about 4 cups)
- 2 medium Italian plum tomatoes, diced
- 2 ounces diced lower-sodium, low-fat ham (about ¼ cup)
- 2 medium green onions, thinly sliced
- 1 tablespoon imitation bacon bits
- ⅛ teaspoon salt
- ¼ teaspoon crushed red pepper flakes

In a large saucepan, bring the broth and carrot to a simmer over medium-high heat. Reduce the heat and simmer, covered, for 5 minutes, or until the carrot is almost tender.

Stir in the remaining ingredients. Increase the heat to medium high and return to a simmer. Reduce the heat and simmer, covered, for 10 minutes, or until the greens are tender and the flavors blend. Ladle into soup bowls.

Per Serving: Calories 61, Total Fat 1.0 g, Saturated Fat 0.0 g, Polyunsaturated Fat 0.0 g, Monounsaturated Fat 0.5 g, Cholesterol 6 mg, Sodium 297 mg, Carbohydrates 7 g, Dietary Fiber 3 g, Sugars 3 g, Protein 7 g

Dietary Exchanges: 1½ Vegetable, ½ Very Lean Meat

BLACK-EYED PEA SOUP

SERVES 4 ▮ *1 cup per serving*

  1 14.5-ounce can fat-free, low-sodium chicken broth
  2 smoked ham hocks (about 1 pound)
 16 ounces frozen black-eyed peas
  1 14.5-ounce can no-salt-added diced tomatoes
 ¼ teaspoon dried thyme, crumbled
 ⅛ teaspoon crushed red pepper flakes
 ¼ teaspoon salt

In a large saucepan, bring the broth to a boil over high heat. Stir in the remaining ingredients except the salt. Return to a boil. Reduce the heat and simmer, covered, for 30 minutes, or until the peas are very tender. Remove from the heat.

Stir in the salt. Let stand for 10 minutes so the flavors blend; the standing time is very important in this recipe. Discard the ham hocks before ladling the soup into soup bowls.

Per Serving: Calories 183, Total Fat 1.0 g, Saturated Fat 0.0 g, Polyunsaturated Fat 0.5 g, Monounsaturated Fat 0.0 g, Cholesterol 0 mg, Sodium 218 mg, Carbohydrates 34 g, Dietary Fiber 7 g, Sugars 3 g, Protein 12 g

Dietary Exchanges: 2 Starch, 1 Vegetable, 1 Very Lean Meat

SWEET POTATO BISQUE

SERVES 4 ▪ *1 cup per serving*

- 2 **cups fat-free, low-sodium chicken broth**
- 1 **13-ounce can sweet potatoes packed with no liquid or in light syrup, drained if needed**
- 1 **medium Red Delicious apple, peeled and cut into bite-size pieces**
- ⅓ **cup firmly packed light brown sugar**
- ¼ **cup fresh orange juice**
- ½ **teaspoon ground cinnamon**
- ½ **cup fat-free or low-fat plain yogurt**

In a medium saucepan, stir together all the ingredients except the yogurt. Bring to a boil over high heat. Reduce the heat and simmer, covered, for 15 minutes, or until the apple is tender.

In a food processor or blender, process the soup in batches until almost smooth. Return the soup to the saucepan. Stir in the yogurt until well blended. Ladle into soup bowls.

Per Serving: Calories 198, Total Fat 0.5 g, Saturated Fat 0.0 g, Polyunsaturated Fat 0.0 g, Monounsaturated Fat 0.0 g, Cholesterol 1 mg, Sodium 102 mg, Carbohydrates 46 g, Dietary Fiber 3 g, Sugars 39 g, Protein 4 g

Dietary Exchanges: 1½ Starch, ½ Fruit, 1 Other Carbohydrate

Tip *A hand blender (immersion blender) is a useful kitchen tool for making soup and other foods silky smooth with ease and without much mess. Simply insert the blender "wand" into the soup and blend the mixture to the desired consistency.*

Salads

ZESTY THREE-BEAN SALAD

SERVES 12 ▮ *½ cup per serving*

- ¼ **cup vinegar**
- 2 **tablespoons honey Dijon mustard**
- 1 **tablespoon honey**
- 2 **teaspoons canola or corn oil**
- 1 **teaspoon celery seeds**
- 1 **medium garlic clove, minced**
- ¼ **teaspoon salt**
- 1 **15-ounce can no-salt-added kidney beans, rinsed and drained**
- 1 **15-ounce can no-salt-added pinto beans, rinsed and drained**
- 1 **14.5-ounce can no-salt-added green beans, drained**
- ⅔ **cup chopped red onion**
- ½ **cup chopped green bell pepper**

In a large resealable plastic bag, thoroughly combine the vinegar, mustard, honey, oil, celery seeds, garlic, and salt. Add the remaining ingredients, seal the bag, and turn gently several times to coat. Refrigerate for at least 2 hours, turning several times, before serving. (Can be prepared a day ahead.)

Per Serving: Calories 90, Total Fat 1.0 g, Saturated Fat 0.0 g, Polyunsaturated Fat 0.0 g, Monounsaturated Fat 0.5 g, Cholesterol 0 mg, Sodium 54 mg, Carbohydrates 16 g, Dietary Fiber 4 g, Sugars 5 g, Protein 5 g

Dietary Exchanges: 1 Starch

CARROT-PINEAPPLE SALAD WITH GOLDEN RAISINS

SERVES 6 ■ *½ cup per serving*

- 2½ cups matchstick-size carrot strips
- 1 8-ounce can pineapple tidbits in their own juice, drained, reserving 1 tablespoon juice
- ⅓ cup golden raisins
- 2 tablespoons sugar
- 2 tablespoons light mayonnaise
- ½ teaspoon curry powder (optional)

In a medium bowl, stir together the carrots, pineapple, and raisins.

In a small bowl, stir together the reserved pineapple juice, sugar, mayonnaise, and curry powder. Pour over the carrot mixture. Stir gently to coat. Spoon into a serving bowl.

Per Serving: Calories 99, Total Fat 2.0 g, Saturated Fat 0.0 g, Polyunsaturated Fat 0.5 g, Monounsaturated Fat 1.0 g, Cholesterol 2 mg, Sodium 81 mg, Carbohydrates 22 g, Dietary Fiber 2 g, Sugars 16 g, Protein 1 g

Dietary Exchanges: 1 Fruit, 1½ Vegetable, ½ Fat

Tip *Even if you think you don't like curry powder, you may want to give it a try in this recipe. The curry powder is subtle, yet really brings the flavors together.*

SWEET-AND-SOUR SLAW

SERVES 4 ■ *½ cup per serving*

- 3 tablespoons red wine vinegar
- 2 tablespoons light brown sugar
- 2 teaspoons olive oil
- 1 teaspoon poppy seeds
- ½ teaspoon onion powder
- 3 cups packaged shredded cabbage and carrot slaw mix
- 1 medium sweet-tart apple, such as Granny Smith, Gala, Fuji, or Golden Delicious, peeled and grated or shredded
- ½ cup thinly sliced red cabbage

In a medium bowl, whisk together the vinegar, brown sugar, oil, poppy seeds, and onion powder. Add the slaw mix, apple, and red cabbage, and toss together thoroughly. Cover and refrigerate for 20 to 30 minutes before serving.

Per Serving: Calories 81, Total Fat 2.5 g, Saturated Fat 0.5 g, Polyunsaturated Fat 0.5 g, Monounsaturated Fat 1.5 g, Cholesterol 0 mg, Sodium 18 mg, Carbohydrates 14 g, Dietary Fiber 2 g, Sugars 12 g, Protein 1 g

Dietary Exchanges: ½ Fruit, 1 Vegetable, ½ Fat

MACARONI SALAD

SERVES 6 ▮ *½ cup per serving*

- **4** ounces dried elbow macaroni
- **¼** cup finely chopped green onions
- **¼** cup fat-free or light sour cream
- **3** tablespoons fat-free or light mayonnaise
- **2** tablespoons sweet pickle relish
- **1** teaspoon spicy brown mustard (lowest sodium available)
- **⅓** cup chopped seeded cucumber
- **⅓** cup chopped celery
- **⅓** cup chopped red bell pepper
- **¼** cup grated carrot

In a medium saucepan, prepare the pasta using the package directions, omitting the salt and oil. Pour into a colander and rinse under cold water. Drain well.

In a medium bowl, stir together the green onions, sour cream, mayonnaise, pickle relish, and mustard. Using a rubber scraper, gently fold in the pasta and remaining ingredients. Cover and refrigerate for 1 to 2 hours, or until well chilled, before serving.

Per Serving: Calories 101, Total Fat 0.5 g, Saturated Fat 0.0 g, Polyunsaturated Fat 0.0 g, Monounsaturated Fat 0.0 g, Cholesterol 3 mg, Sodium 138 mg, Carbohydrates 20 g, Dietary Fiber 2 g, Sugars 3 g, Protein 3 g

Dietary Exchanges: 1½ Starch

The Power Is In Your Hands

Stroke and heart disease are major health risks for everyone, especially for African Americans. But you have the power to take charge of your health by making good choices.

KNOW YOUR RISKS

Those good choices start with good information. Learn about the factors that increase your risk for cardiovascular disease and what you can do about them. Some factors—such as increasing age and family history—can't be changed, but many can. **You have the power to affect these major risk factors: smoking, high blood pressure, high blood cholesterol, diabetes, obesity, and physical inactivity.** Get screened to find out if you're at risk. (To start, take the quiz on page 26.) If you are at risk, work with your doctor to decide what actions you should take to reduce your risk.

DON'T SMOKE OR BREATHE TOBACCO SMOKE

Smoking or breathing tobacco smoke is the single greatest cause of preventable death among African Americans in the United States. Smoking greatly increases your risk of cardiovascular disease. The good news is that when you do stop smoking—no matter how long or how much you've smoked—your risk of heart disease and stroke drops rapidly. One to two years after you quit, your risk of coronary heart disease is substantially reduced.

American Heart Association® | American Stroke Association®

POWER TO END STROKE℠
You are the Power

If you don't smoke, don't start. If you do smoke, stop now! **You have the power to quit.** Ask your doctor to suggest a smoking cessation program that will work for you.

WATCH YOUR BLOOD PRESSURE

High blood pressure (hypertension) is often called the silent killer because it has no symptoms. It affects more than 42 percent of adult non-Hispanic black men and nearly 47 percent of women. Compared to whites, African Americans are more likely to have high blood pressure, develop it earlier in life, and have more severe cases.

Have your blood pressure checked at least once every two years—more often if you have a family history of high blood pressure, stroke, or heart attack. In between visits to your doctor, you can also check your blood pressure at your local drugstore. The first number (systolic pressure) measures the force of blood in your arteries when your heart beats. The second number (diastolic pressure) is the force while your heart rests between beats. Compare your results with the chart below to see if you're at risk. If your readings are in the prehypertension or high categories, work with your doctor to lower your blood pressure.

Blood Pressure	Normal	Prehypertension	High
Systolic (mm Hg)	Less than 120	120 to 139	140 or higher
Diastolic (mm Hg)	Less than 80	80 to 89	90 or higher

KNOW YOUR BLOOD CHOLESTEROL LEVELS

Cholesterol is a fatlike substance produced by your liver. Cholesterol is also present in foods from animals (especially egg yolks, meat, poultry, seafood, and whole and 2 percent dairy products). Excess cholesterol can form plaque on the inner wall of your arteries, making it harder for your heart to circulate blood. Plaque can break open and cause blood clots. If a clot blocks an artery that feeds the brain, it causes a stroke. If it blocks an artery that feeds the heart, it causes a heart attack.

Among non-Hispanic blacks age 20 and older, nearly 45 percent of men and about 42 percent of women have total blood cholesterol levels of 200 mg/dL or higher. Are you one of them? **Get a simple blood test to find out if your blood cholesterol level is desirable, is borderline-high, or puts you at high risk of developing heart disease and stroke** (see the chart below). Contact your local American Heart Association to find out about free or low-cost screenings in your community.

Talk to your doctor about managing high blood cholesterol. Eating a healthful diet and being more physically active are good ways to start. If your cholesterol stays high, you may need medication to help reduce your risk. Be sure to take medication as prescribed, and talk to your doctor before you stop taking it.

Cholesterol Level (mg/dL)	Desirable (low risk)	Borderline-High Risk	High Risk
Total cholesterol	Less than 200	200 to 239	240 or higher
LDL ("bad") cholesterol	Less than 130*	130 to 159	160 or higher
HDL ("good") cholesterol	40 or higher for men; 50 or higher for women**		Less than 40 for men; less than 50 for women

*People who have had an ischemic stroke or heart attack (or are at risk for having one) may be advised by their doctor to keep their LDL level below 100, or if they're at very high risk, below 70 mg/dL.
**The higher, the better—an HDL level of 60 mg/dL and above is considered protective against heart disease.

MONITOR FOR DIABETES

Most of the food we eat turns into glucose, or sugar, for our bodies to use for energy. The hormone insulin helps glucose enter the cells of the body. When you have diabetes, your body doesn't make enough insulin or can't use its own insulin as well as it should, or both. This results in increased blood levels of glucose.

Diabetes is very common in the African American community, but many people don't even know they have it. **Have your glucose levels checked regularly, especially if you have a family history of diabetes.** People with diabetes often also have high blood pressure and high blood cholesterol and are overweight, further increasing their risk for heart disease and stroke.

An oral glucose tolerance test reading of 200 or more or a fasting plasma test reading of 126 or more, measured on at least two occasions, indicates that you may have diabetes. An oral glucose tolerance test reading of 140 to 199 or a fasting plasma test reading of 100 to 125 indicates a condition called prediabetes. If your glucose level falls in either category, consult your doctor to learn how to monitor and prevent or manage diabetes.

AIM FOR A HEALTHY WEIGHT

Obesity is a major concern for all Americans, including African Americans. You have a much higher risk of heart disease and stroke if you're overweight or obese, even if you have no other risk factors. Excess body fat—especially at your waist—raises blood pressure and blood cholesterol levels and increases your risk of developing diabetes.

You often can decrease your risk of heart disease and stroke by losing as little as 10 to 20 pounds. Establish a sensible eating and physical activity plan that will help you reach and maintain a healthy weight. Avoid fad diets and promotions that promise you will lose weight quickly. You don't gain weight overnight, so don't expect to lose it that way and keep it off for the long term. Obesity is not an appearance issue; it's a health issue. Whether you like the way you look or not, you owe it to yourself to develop a healthy lifestyle.

BE PHYSICALLY ACTIVE

It's well known that being physically active improves your cardiovascular fitness, but you may not realize that consistent inactivity actually increases your risk for heart disease and stroke.

Make your goal at least 30 minutes of physical activity on most, if not all, days of the week. Being physically active can help you prevent or control high blood pressure, high blood cholesterol, diabetes, and obesity and overweight. Exercise can also help you reduce stress levels, give you more energy, and improve your self-image. Choose an activity that you enjoy, set reasonable short- and long-term goals, and remember to reward yourself along the way as you achieve your goals.

LEARN THE WARNING SIGNS AND TAKE THE PLEDGE

Learn to recognize the warning signs of stroke, listed below. Acting quickly when these signs occur can mean the difference between survival and disability or death. Share this information with your loved ones to show you care.

JOIN THE MOVEMENT!

Show your commitment: Take the pledge. Then tear out this page and post it where you will be reminded that you have the power to end stroke.

I'm real. I'm strong. I'm proud. But I'm at risk for stroke.

The American Stroke Association is ready to talk to me about what matters—to me.

They can meet me where I am—to make positive lifestyle changes.

They can make a positive impact—on me and my legacy.

So I pledge...

To not just survive—but thrive. I will learn how to live stronger and longer—for me, my family, and my community. I will join the movement to prevent and overcome stroke.

I will call 9-1-1 immediately if I or someone I know experiences these signs of stroke:

- **Sudden numbness or weakness of the face, arm, or leg, especially on one side of the body**
- **Sudden confusion or trouble speaking or understanding**
- **Sudden trouble seeing in one or both eyes**
- **Sudden trouble walking, dizziness, or loss of balance or coordination**
- **Sudden severe headache with no known cause**

Signature _____ Date _____

Call **1-888-4-STROKE** or visit **StrokeAssociation.org/power** for more information.

TAKE THE RISK ASSESSMENT QUIZ

You don't have to become a statistic! You have the power to reduce your risk of heart disease and stroke. The quiz that follows will help you see where you need to focus your efforts. Then work with your doctor to prevent, reduce, or control as many risk factors as you can.

✔ Check all that apply to you. If you check two or more, please see your doctor for a complete assessment of your risk.

AGE

☐ You are a man over 45 or a woman over 55 years old.

FAMILY HISTORY

☐ You have a close blood relative who had a heart attack or stroke before age 55 (if father or brother) or before age 65 (if mother or sister).

MEDICAL HISTORY

☐ You have coronary artery disease or you have had a heart attack.

☐ You have had a stroke.

☐ You have an abnormal heartbeat.

TOBACCO SMOKE

☐ You smoke or you live or work with people who smoke every day.

BLOOD PRESSURE

☐ Your blood pressure is 140/90 mm Hg or higher, or you've been told that your blood pressure is too high.

☐ You don't know what your blood pressure is.

TOTAL CHOLESTEROL AND HDL CHOLESTEROL

☐ Your total cholesterol level is 240 mg/dL or higher.

☐ Your HDL ("good") cholesterol level is less than 40 mg/dL if you're a man or less than 50 mg/dL if you're a woman.

☐ You don't know your total cholesterol or HDL levels.

PHYSICAL INACTIVITY

☐ You don't accumulate at least 30 minutes of physical activity on most days of the week.

EXCESS BODY WEIGHT

☐ You are 20 pounds or more overweight.

DIABETES

☐ You have diabetes or take medicine to control your blood sugar.

KEEP TRACK OF YOUR NUMBERS

Each time you visit your doctor, use a log like this one to record your blood pressure, blood cholesterol, and blood glucose.

Date	Blood Pressure	Cholesterol			Blood Glucose
		LDL	HDL	Total	

Physical activity can help manage risk factors such as high blood pressure, obesity, and diabetes. Use this sample log to track all the ways you fit exercise into your day at home or at work. If you have a health condition or haven't been active for a long time, talk with your doctor before starting any new exercise program. Remember to start out slowly and increase your activity over time.

Date	Home (How Long)	Work (How Long)	Play (How Long)	Total Time
July 16	Walked the dog (30 mins)	Climbed stairs to 3rd floor twice (10 mins)	Played basketball with Joe (40 mins)	1 hr 20 mins

Seafood

CRAB CAKES

SERVES 4 ▓ *2 crab cakes and 1 tablespoon sauce per serving*

- 1   6-ounce can lump crabmeat, drained
- ½   cup shredded carrots
- ¼   cup plain dry bread crumbs
- 2   medium green onions, thinly sliced
-     Whites of 2 large eggs, lightly beaten
- 1   tablespoon fat-free or light mayonnaise
- 1   teaspoon salt-free Cajun or Creole seasoning blend *(see tip on page 78)*
- ¼   cup plain dry bread crumbs
- 2   teaspoons olive oil
- 3   tablespoons fat-free or low-fat sour cream
- 1   tablespoon fat-free or light mayonnaise
- 2   teaspoons fresh lemon juice
- 2   teaspoons bottled white horseradish
- ⅛   teaspoon paprika (optional)

In a medium bowl, stir together the crabmeat, carrots, ¼ cup bread crumbs, green onions, egg whites, 1 tablespoon mayonnaise, and seasoning blend.

To shape the crab cakes easily, spread the remaining ¼ cup bread crumbs on a dinner plate. Place a 2-inch round cookie cutter or biscuit cutter on the plate. Spoon about 2 tablespoons crab mixture into the cookie cutter. Using a spoon, gently press the mixture down into the cutter. Sprinkle a small amount of the bread crumbs on top of the crab mixture. Carefully remove the cutter and place it on a different space on the plate. Repeat with the remaining crab mixture and bread crumbs until you have 8 crab cakes.

Heat the oil in a large nonstick skillet over medium heat, swirling to coat the bottom. Cook the crab cakes for 2 to 3 minutes on each side, or until they are golden brown and cooked through.

Meanwhile, in a small bowl, stir together the remaining ingredients except the paprika.

To serve, put 2 crab cakes on each plate. Spoon 1½ teaspoons sauce over each crab cake. Sprinkle with the paprika.

Per Serving: Calories 151, Total Fat 4.0 g, Saturated Fat 0.5 g, Polyunsaturated Fat 0.5 g, Monounsaturated Fat 2.0 g, Cholesterol 33 mg, Sodium 371 mg, Carbohydrates 16 g, Dietary Fiber 2 g, Sugars 4 g, Protein 14 g

Dietary Exchanges: 1 Starch, 1½ Lean Meat

FISH STEW WITH TOMATOES

SERVES 4 ▪ *1¼ cups per serving*

- 1 teaspoon canola or corn oil
- 1 medium green bell pepper, chopped
- 1 medium carrot, quartered lengthwise and chopped
- ½ medium onion, chopped
- 1 6-ounce baking potato, peeled and diced
- 1 14.5-ounce can no-salt-added diced tomatoes, undrained
- 1 cup water
- 1 teaspoon salt-free Cajun or Creole seasoning blend *(see tip on page 78)*
- 3 tilapia, catfish, or other mild white fish fillets (about 4 ounces each)
- 2 teaspoons light tub margarine
- ½ teaspoon salt

In a Dutch oven, heat the oil over medium-high heat, swirling to coat the bottom. Cook the bell pepper, carrot, and onion for 4 minutes, or until the onion is soft, stirring frequently. Stir in the potato, undrained tomatoes, water, and seasoning blend. Bring to a boil. Reduce the heat and simmer, covered, for 20 minutes, or until the potato pieces are tender.

Meanwhile, rinse the fish and pat dry with paper towels. Cut the fish into 1-inch squares. When the potato pieces are tender, add the fish. Gently stir. Cook, covered, for 5 minutes, or until the fish flakes easily when tested with a fork. Remove from the heat.

Fold in the margarine and salt, being careful not to break up the fish. Let stand, covered, for 5 minutes so the flavors blend. Ladle into soup bowls.

Per Serving: Calories 171, Total Fat 3.5 g, Saturated Fat 0.5 g, Polyunsaturated Fat 1.0 g, Monounsaturated Fat 0.5 g, Cholesterol 36 mg, Sodium 399 mg, Carbohydrates 17 g, Dietary Fiber 4 g, Sugars 6 g, Protein 19 g

Dietary Exchanges: ½ Starch, 2 Vegetable, 2 Lean Meat

SHRIMP AND GRITS

SERVES 4 ■ *1 cup per serving*

- 8 ounces peeled raw medium shrimp, thawed if frozen
- 2 tablespoons water
- ½ teaspoon seafood seasoning blend
- 1 teaspoon canola or corn oil
- 1 medium red bell pepper, finely chopped
- 1 medium green bell pepper, finely chopped
- 5 medium green onions, chopped
- 2 cups fat-free milk
- ½ cup uncooked quick-cooking grits
- ¼ teaspoon salt
- ½ cup shredded reduced-fat sharp Cheddar cheese
- 1 teaspoon Worcestershire sauce (lowest sodium available)
- ½ teaspoon seafood seasoning blend

Heat a medium nonstick skillet over medium heat. Cook the shrimp, water, and ½ teaspoon seasoning blend for 5 minutes, or until the shrimp turn pink on the outside and are opaque in the center, stirring frequently. Pour into a bowl.

In the same skillet, heat the oil, swirling to coat the bottom. Cook the bell peppers and green onions for 5 minutes, or until tender, stirring frequently. Stir in the milk, grits, and salt. Increase the heat to medium high and bring to a boil. Reduce the heat and simmer, covered, for 5 minutes, or until thickened, stirring occasionally. Remove from the heat.

Stir in the Cheddar, Worcestershire sauce, remaining seasoning blend, and shrimp with any accumulated liquid. Cover and let stand for 5 minutes so the flavors blend, the shrimp warm, and the cheese melts.

Per Serving: Calories 218, Total Fat 3.0 g, Saturated Fat 1.0 g, Polyunsaturated Fat 0.5 g, Monounsaturated Fat 1.0 g, Cholesterol 89 mg, Sodium 540 mg, Carbohydrates 28 g, Dietary Fiber 3 g, Sugars 10 g, Protein 19 g

Dietary Exchanges: 1 Starch, 1½ Vegetable, ½ Skim Milk, 2 Very Lean Meat

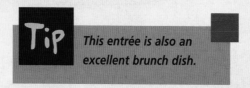

Tip *This entrée is also an excellent brunch dish.*

BLACKENED REDFISH

SERVES 4 ■ *3 ounces fish per serving*

- **1 tablespoon fresh lime juice**
- **2 teaspoons olive oil**
- **1 pound redfish, cut into 4 pieces, rinsed and patted dry with paper towels**
- **1 teaspoon chili powder**
- **½ teaspoon dried thyme, crumbled**
- **½ teaspoon ground cumin**
- **½ teaspoon onion powder**
- **½ teaspoon garlic powder**
- **¼ teaspoon salt**
- **1 teaspoon olive oil**

In a shallow bowl, stir together the lime juice and 2 teaspoons oil. Add the fish and turn to coat. Cover and marinate for 5 to 10 minutes at room temperature or for up to 1 hour in the refrigerator, turning once.

Meanwhile, in a small bowl, stir together the remaining ingredients except the 1 teaspoon oil.

Remove the fish from the marinade, letting the excess marinade drip back into the bowl. Transfer the fish to a large plate and discard the marinade. Sprinkle half the chili powder mixture over the top side of the fish.

Heat the remaining oil in a large nonstick skillet over medium-high heat, swirling to coat the bottom. Cook the fish with the seasoned side down for 4 minutes. Sprinkle the top side with the remaining chili powder mixture. Turn and cook the fish for 3 to 4 minutes, or until it flakes easily when tested with a fork. Transfer to plates.

Per Serving: Calories 150, Total Fat 7.0 g, Saturated Fat 1.5 g, Polyunsaturated Fat 1.5 g, Monounsaturated Fat 3.5 g, Cholesterol 73 mg, Sodium 231 mg, Carbohydrates 1 g, Dietary Fiber 0 g, Sugars 0 g, Protein 20 g

Dietary Exchanges: 3 Lean Meat

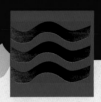

TUNA NOODLE SUPPER

SERVES 4 ▓ *1½ cups per serving*

- 2 **cups dried whole-wheat rotini (about 6 ounces)**
- ¼ **cup plain dry bread crumbs**
- 2 **tablespoons sliced almonds**
- 2 **teaspoons olive oil**
- 1 **pound sliced button or baby portobello mushrooms, or a combination**
- 1 **cup fat-free milk**
- 1 **cup fat-free, low-sodium chicken broth**
- 2 **tablespoons all-purpose flour**
- ¼ **teaspoon salt**
- ¼ **teaspoon pepper**
- 1 **12-ounce can tuna in distilled or spring water, rinsed, drained, and flaked**
- ¼ **cup shredded or grated Parmesan cheese**

Prepare the pasta using the package directions, omitting the salt and oil. Drain well in a colander. Set aside.

Meanwhile, in a large nonstick skillet, cook the bread crumbs and nuts over medium-high heat for 1 minute, or until just beginning to brown, stirring constantly. Transfer to a small plate.

In the same skillet, heat the oil over medium-high heat, swirling to coat the bottom. Cook the mushrooms for 5 to 6 minutes, or until tender, stirring occasionally.

In a small bowl, whisk together the milk, broth, flour, salt, and pepper. Pour into the mushrooms, stirring to combine. Bring to a simmer. Cook for 2 to 3 minutes, or until thickened, stirring occasionally. Stir in the tuna and Parmesan. Cook for 2 minutes, or until warmed through, stirring occasionally. Stir in the pasta. Cook for 1 minute, or until warmed through, stirring occasionally. Sprinkle with the bread crumbs and almonds. Spoon onto plates.

Per Serving: Calories 404, Total Fat 9.0 g, Saturated Fat 2.5 g, Polyunsaturated Fat 2.0 g, Monounsaturated Fat 4.0 g, Cholesterol 41 mg, Sodium 410 mg, Carbohydrates 47 g, Dietary Fiber 7 g, Sugars 7 g, Protein 36 g

Dietary Exchanges: 3 Starch, 4 Lean Meat

Poultry

HOPPIN' JOHN

SERVES 4 ■ *1 cup per serving*

- ½ cup uncooked instant brown or white rice
- 1 teaspoon canola or corn oil
- 3 ounces low-fat smoked turkey sausage ring (lowest fat and sodium available), quartered lengthwise and cut into ¼-inch pieces
- ½ medium red bell pepper, finely chopped
- 1 medium jalapeño, seeded and finely chopped (wear plastic gloves when handling)
- 1 15-ounce can no-salt-added black-eyed peas, rinsed and drained
- ½ cup water
- ¼ teaspoon salt

Prepare the rice using the package directions, omitting the salt and margarine.

Meanwhile, in a medium nonstick skillet, heat the oil over medium-high heat, swirling to coat the bottom. Cook the sausage for 3 minutes, or until richly browned, stirring frequently. Stir in the bell pepper and jalapeño. Cook for 1 minute. Stir in the peas, water, and salt. Cook for 2 minutes, or until the mixture is thickened slightly but some liquid remains. Remove from the heat.

Let stand, covered, for 5 minutes so the flavors blend. Stir in the rice. Transfer to a serving bowl.

Per Serving: Calories 182, Total Fat 4.0 g, Saturated Fat 1.0 g, Polyunsaturated Fat 1.0 g, Monounsaturated Fat 2.0 g, Cholesterol 14 mg, Sodium 350 mg, Carbohydrates 27 g, Dietary Fiber 5 g, Sugars 5 g, Protein 10 g

Dietary Exchanges: 2 Starch, 1 Very Lean Meat

HOT-WING-FLAVORED CHICKEN WITH RANCH SAUCE

SERVES 4 ▓ *3 ounces chicken and 2 tablespoons sauce per serving*

- 2 tablespoons hot-pepper sauce, or to taste
- 1 tablespoon fresh lemon juice
- 2 teaspoons olive oil
- 4 boneless, skinless chicken breast halves (about 4 ounces each), all visible fat discarded
  Vegetable oil spray
- 1 cup cornflake crumbs (about 2 cups flakes)
- ¼ cup fat-free or light sour cream
- ¼ cup low-fat buttermilk
- ½ teaspoon garlic powder
- ¼ teaspoon dried dillweed, crumbled

In a large shallow bowl, stir together the hot-pepper sauce, lemon juice, and olive oil. Add the chicken and turn to coat. Cover and refrigerate for 30 minutes to 8 hours, turning occasionally if longer than 30 minutes. Discard the marinade.

Preheat the oven to 375°F. Lightly spray an 8-inch square baking pan with vegetable oil spray.

Put the cornflake crumbs on a plate. Turn the chicken to coat both sides. Transfer to the baking pan. Lightly spray the top of the chicken with vegetable oil spray. Bake for 30 minutes, or until the chicken is no longer pink in the center and the coating is crisp. Transfer to a serving plate.

Meanwhile, in a small bowl, whisk together the remaining ingredients. Cover and refrigerate until ready to serve. Spoon the sauce over the chicken or use as a dipping sauce.

Per Serving: Calories 220, Total Fat 4.0 g, Saturated Fat 1.0 g, Polyunsaturated Fat 0.5 g, Monounsaturated Fat 2.0 g, Cholesterol 69 mg, Sodium 250 mg, Carbohydrates 16 g, Dietary Fiber 1 g, Sugars 3 g, Protein 29 g

Dietary Exchanges: 1 Starch, 3 Very Lean Meat

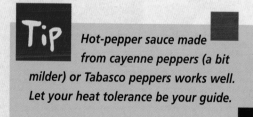

Tip *Hot-pepper sauce made from cayenne peppers (a bit milder) or Tabasco peppers works well. Let your heat tolerance be your guide.*

CHICKEN SPAGHETTI

SERVES 4 ■ *1½ cups per serving*

Vegetable oil spray

4 ounces dried whole-wheat spaghetti

1 teaspoon olive oil

1 medium red bell pepper, thinly sliced

1 medium green bell pepper, thinly sliced

½ medium onion, chopped

2 cups diced skinless cooked chicken breast, cooked without salt (about 8 ounces)

1 14.5-ounce can no-salt-added diced tomatoes, undrained

1 10.75-ounce can low-fat, reduced-sodium condensed cream of chicken soup

½ cup reduced-fat shredded Cheddar cheese

¼ cup shredded or grated Parmesan cheese

¼ teaspoon pepper

Preheat the oven to 350°F. Lightly spray an 8-inch square baking dish with vegetable oil spray.

Prepare the spaghetti using the package directions, omitting the salt and oil. Drain well in a colander.

Meanwhile, in a large skillet, heat the oil over medium heat, swirling to coat the bottom. Cook the bell peppers and onion for 4 to 5 minutes, or until tender, stirring occasionally. Pour into a large bowl. Stir in the remaining ingredients except the spaghetti. Stir in the spaghetti. Pour into the baking dish.

Bake, covered, for 20 minutes. Bake, uncovered, for 10 minutes, or until the mixture is warmed through and light golden brown on top.

Per Serving: Calories 371, Total Fat 9.0 g, Saturated Fat 4.0 g, Polyunsaturated Fat 1.0 g, Monounsaturated Fat 3.0 g, Cholesterol 75 mg, Sodium 544 mg, Carbohydrates 39 g, Dietary Fiber 7 g, Sugars 8 g, Protein 35 g

Dietary Exchanges: 2 Starch, 2 Vegetable, 4 Lean Meat

CHICKEN JAMBALAYA

SERVES 4 ▓ *1½ cups per serving*

> Vegetable oil spray
> 4 ounces low-fat smoked sausage (lowest fat and sodium available), cut into bite-size pieces
> 1 medium onion, chopped
> 12 ounces boneless, skinless chicken breasts, all visible fat discarded, cut into bite-size pieces
> ½ medium red bell pepper, chopped
> ½ medium green bell pepper, chopped
> ¾ cup uncooked long-grain rice
> 3 medium garlic cloves, minced
> 1 teaspoon salt-free extra-spicy seasoning blend
> ½ teaspoon dried thyme, crumbled
> ½ teaspoon dried oregano, crumbled
> 1 14.5-ounce can no-salt-added diced tomatoes, undrained
> ¾ cup fat-free, low-sodium chicken broth
> Red hot-pepper sauce (optional)

Lightly spray a Dutch oven with vegetable oil spray. Heat over medium-high heat. Cook the sausage and onion for 2 to 3 minutes, or until the onion is soft, stirring constantly. Stir in the chicken and bell peppers. Cook for 4 minutes, or until the chicken is no longer pink on the outside, stirring frequently. Reduce the heat to medium low. Stir in the rice, garlic, seasoning blend, thyme, and oregano. Cook for 2 minutes, stirring frequently. Stir in the undrained tomatoes and broth. Increase the heat to high and bring to a boil. Reduce the heat and simmer, covered, for 20 minutes, or until the rice is thoroughly cooked.

Ladle into bowls. Serve with the hot-pepper sauce.

Per Serving: Calories 302, Total Fat 4.0 g, Saturated Fat 1.0 g, Polyunsaturated Fat 1.0 g, Monounsaturated Fat 1.5 g, Cholesterol 68 mg, Sodium 378 mg, Carbohydrates 38 g, Dietary Fiber 3 g, Sugars 7 g, Protein 28 g

Dietary Exchanges: 2 Starch, 1½ Vegetable, 3 Very Lean Meat

PAN-SEARED JERK CHICKEN

SERVES 4 ■ *3 ounces chicken per serving*

- **1** teaspoon olive oil
- **4** boneless, skinless chicken breast halves (about 4 ounces each), all visible fat discarded
- **1** teaspoon jerk seasoning blend
- **½** teaspoon paprika
- **½** teaspoon sugar
- **1** teaspoon olive oil
- **½** medium lime
- **½** teaspoon grated lime zest
- **⅛** teaspoon salt

Rub 1 teaspoon oil over both sides of the chicken.

In a small bowl, stir together the seasoning blend, paprika, and sugar. Sprinkle over both sides of the chicken. Using your fingertips, gently press the mixture so it adheres to the chicken.

In a large nonstick skillet, heat 1 teaspoon oil over medium-high heat, swirling to coat the bottom. Cook the chicken for 4 minutes. Turn and cook for 5 minutes, or until no longer pink in the center. Remove the skillet from the heat.

Squeeze the lime over the chicken. Sprinkle with the lime zest. Let stand in the skillet for 3 minutes so the chicken releases its juices, dissolving any browned bits in the skillet. Stir the chicken around in the skillet to coat it in the concentrated pan drippings. Sprinkle with the salt. Transfer the chicken to plates.

Per Serving: Calories 149, Total Fat 3.5 g, Saturated Fat 0.5 g, Polyunsaturated Fat 0.5 g, Monounsaturated Fat 2.0 g, Cholesterol 66 mg, Sodium 147 mg, Carbohydrates 1 g, Dietary Fiber 0 g, Sugars 1 g, Protein 26 g

Dietary Exchanges: 3 Lean Meat

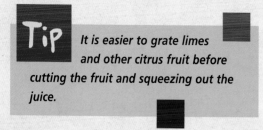

Tip *It is easier to grate limes and other citrus fruit before cutting the fruit and squeezing out the juice.*

SMOTHERED CHICKEN

SERVES 4 ▪ *3 ounces chicken plus 2 tablespoons sauce per serving*

- ¼ **teaspoon dried thyme, crumbled**
- ¼ **teaspoon paprika**
- ¼ **teaspoon salt**
- ⅛ **teaspoon pepper**
- 4 **boneless, skinless chicken breast halves (about 4 ounces each), all visible fat discarded**
- 1 **tablespoon all-purpose flour**
- 1 **teaspoon canola or corn oil**
- 1 **14.5-ounce can fat-free, low-sodium chicken broth**
- 2 **tablespoons fat-free milk**

In a small bowl, stir together the thyme, paprika, salt, and pepper. Sprinkle over the smooth side of the chicken.

Heat a medium nonstick skillet over medium-high heat. Cook the flour for 1½ to 2 minutes, or until beginning to turn light golden, stirring constantly. Do not overcook. Transfer to a small bowl.

In the same skillet, heat the oil, swirling to coat the bottom. Cook the chicken with the seasoned side down for 1 minute, or until beginning to brown. Increase the heat to high. Pour in the broth and bring to a boil. Reduce the heat and simmer, covered, for 12 minutes, or until the chicken is no longer pink in the center. Transfer the chicken with the browned side up to a serving plate. Cover with aluminum foil to keep warm.

Increase the heat to high and bring the broth to a boil. Boil for 5 minutes, or until the liquid is reduced to about ¾ cup.

Meanwhile, whisk the milk into the cooked flour until well blended. Whisk into the reduced broth. Cook over high heat for 2 minutes, or until well blended and thickened slightly, whisking constantly. Spoon the sauce over the chicken.

Per Serving: Calories 150, Total Fat 2.5 g, Saturated Fat 0.5 g, Polyunsaturated Fat 0.5 g, Monounsaturated Fat 1.0 g, Cholesterol 66 mg, Sodium 248 mg, Carbohydrates 2 g, Dietary Fiber 0 g, Sugars 0 g, Protein 28 g

Dietary Exchanges: 3 Very Lean Meat

Meats

SLOW-SIMMERED BEEF POT

SERVES 4 ▌ *1 cup per serving*

     Vegetable oil spray
1 teaspoon canola or corn oil
1 pound top round steak, all visible fat discarded, cut into 1-inch cubes
1 medium onion, cut lengthwise into eighths
1 cup water
1½ teaspoons instant coffee granules
¼ teaspoon pepper
3 medium carrots, cut crosswise into 2-inch pieces
1 medium green bell pepper and 1 medium red bell pepper, or
    2 medium green bell peppers, cut into 1-inch squares
2 tablespoons no-salt-added ketchup
1 tablespoon Italian salad dressing mix (about ½ 0.7-ounce packet)

Lightly spray a Dutch oven with vegetable oil spray. Pour in the oil, swirling to coat the bottom. Heat over medium-high heat. Cook the steak for 3 to 4 minutes, or until beginning to brown, stirring frequently. Stir in the onion, water, coffee granules, and pepper. Increase the heat to high and bring to a boil. Reduce the heat and simmer, covered, for 45 minutes, or until the beef just begins to become slightly tender (no stirring needed).

Stir in the remaining ingredients. Increase the heat to high and bring to a boil. Reduce the heat and simmer, covered, for 30 minutes, or until the beef is very tender (no stirring needed).

Per Serving: Calories 216, Total Fat 5.0 g, Saturated Fat 1.5 g, Polyunsaturated Fat 0.5 g, Monounsaturated Fat 2.0 g, Cholesterol 64 mg, Sodium 472 mg, Carbohydrates 15 g, Dietary Fiber 3 g, Sugars 9 g, Protein 27 g

Dietary Exchanges: 3 Vegetable, 3 Lean Meat

Tip If you wish, serve this dish beside or over no-yolk egg noodles.

GARLIC PORK ROAST

SERVES 8 ▓ *3 ounces pork and 2 tablespoons onion mixture per serving*

> Vegetable oil spray
> 1 2-pound boneless top loin pork roast (not tenderloin), all visible fat discarded
> 4 medium garlic cloves, halved lengthwise
> ½ teaspoon pepper (coarsely ground preferred)
> ½ teaspoon paprika
> 2 teaspoons olive oil, divided use
> 3 medium onions (about 12 ounces), thinly sliced
> ¼ teaspoon salt
> ¼ cup water
> ¼ teaspoon salt

Preheat the oven to 325°F. Lightly spray an 11×7×2-inch baking pan with vegetable oil spray.

Using a paring knife, make 8 small, widely spaced slits in the pork. Place half a garlic clove in each. Sprinkle the pepper and paprika over the pork. Using your fingertips, gently press the pepper and paprika so they adhere to the pork.

In a large nonstick skillet, heat 1 teaspoon oil over medium-high heat, swirling to coat the bottom. Cook the pork for 2 minutes on each side, or until richly browned. Transfer to the baking pan. Set aside.

In the same skillet, heat the remaining 1 teaspoon oil over medium-high heat, swirling to coat the bottom. Scrape to dislodge any browned bits. Cook the onions and ¼ teaspoon salt for 7 minutes, or until the onions are richly browned, stirring frequently. Pour the water into the skillet. Stir. Spoon the mixture around the pork in the baking pan. Sprinkle the pork with the remaining salt.

Bake, covered, for 1 hour 15 minutes, or until the internal temperature registers 155°F on a meat or instant-read thermometer. Transfer the pork to a cutting board. Let stand for 10 minutes so the pork will continue to cook. Slice. Serve with the onion mixture.

Per Serving: Calories 163, Total Fat 5.0 g, Saturated Fat 1.5 g, Polyunsaturated Fat 0.5 g, Monounsaturated Fat 2.5 g, Cholesterol 56 mg, Sodium 289 mg, Carbohydrates 6 g, Dietary Fiber 1 g, Sugars 3 g, Protein 22 g

Dietary Exchanges: 1 Vegetable, 3 Lean Meat

HONEY-BARBECUE PORK CHOPS

SERVES 4 ▮ *1 pork chop per serving*

- ¼ cup mesquite- or hickory-smoked barbecue sauce (lowest sodium available)
- 3 tablespoons honey
- ½ teaspoon ground cumin
- ¼ teaspoon salt
- ⅛ teaspoon pepper
- 4 very thin pork loin chops with bone (about 1 pound 4 ounces), all visible fat discarded
- 1 teaspoon canola or corn oil

In a small bowl, stir together the barbecue sauce, honey, and cumin.

Sprinkle the salt and pepper over both sides of the pork chops. In a large nonstick skillet, heat the oil over medium-high heat, swirling to coat the bottom. Cook the pork chops for 2 minutes. Spoon half the sauce over the pork chops. Turn the pork chops. Spoon the remaining sauce over the pork chops. Cook for 2 minutes. Reduce the heat to medium. Turn the pork chops. Cook for 1 minute on each side, moving the pork chops around in the skillet to coat with the sauce, which darkens to a rich brown as it cooks.

Per Serving: Calories 224, Total Fat 9.0 g, Saturated Fat 3.0 g, Polyunsaturated Fat 1.0 g, Monounsaturated Fat 4.0 g, Cholesterol 49 mg, Sodium 293 mg, Carbohydrates 20 g, Dietary Fiber 0 g, Sugars 19 g, Protein 15 g

Dietary Exchanges: 1½ Other Carbohydrate, 2 Medium-Fat Meat

COUNTRY-FRIED STEAK WITH CREAMY GRAVY

SERVES 4 ■ *3 ounces steak and 2 tablespoons gravy per serving*

- ½ cup low-fat buttermilk
- ⅓ cup all-purpose flour
- 2 teaspoons salt-free extra-spicy seasoning blend
- ⅛ teaspoon salt
- 1 1-pound top round cube steak, cut into 4 pieces
- 2 teaspoons canola or corn oil

Creamy Gravy

- ¼ cup all-purpose flour
- 2 teaspoons salt-free powdered chicken bouillon or very low sodium chicken granules
- ⅛ teaspoon salt (omit if using chicken granules)
- 2 cups fat-free milk
- 1 tablespoon Worcestershire sauce (lowest sodium available)
- 1 teaspoon chipotle pepper sauce or red hot-pepper sauce

Pour the buttermilk into a shallow bowl. In a separate shallow bowl, stir together the flour, seasoning blend, and ⅛ teaspoon salt. Set the bowls and a large plate in a row, assembly-line fashion. Dip a steak in the buttermilk, turning to coat. Put the steak in the flour mixture, turning to coat. Gently shake off the excess flour. Put the steak on the plate. Repeat with the remaining steaks.

In a large nonstick skillet, heat the oil over medium-high heat, swirling to coat the bottom. Cook the steaks for 5 to 6 minutes on each side, or until browned, being careful when turning so the coating does not stick to the skillet. Transfer to a large plate.

Meanwhile, in a small bowl, stir together the flour, bouillon, and ⅛ teaspoon salt if using. Gradually pour in the milk, whisking until smooth. Whisk in the Worcestershire sauce and pepper sauce. When the steaks are removed from the skillet, pour this mixture in. Increase the heat to high and bring to a boil, stirring often. Reduce the heat and simmer for 3 to 5 minutes, or until thickened. Add the steaks, spooning the gravy over them. Simmer, covered, for 5 minutes. Transfer the steaks and gravy to plates.

Per Serving: Calories 290, Total Fat 6.5 g, Saturated Fat 1.5 g, Polyunsaturated Fat 1.0 g, Monounsaturated Fat 3.0 g, Cholesterol 67 mg, Sodium 271 mg, Carbohydrates 23 g, Dietary Fiber 1 g, Sugars 8 g, Protein 33 g

Dietary Exchanges: 1 Starch, ½ Skim Milk, 3 Lean Meat

Vegetarian Entrées

VEGETABLE GUMBO

SERVES 4 ▮ ¾ cup gumbo and ½ cup rice per serving

- 2 tablespoons all-purpose flour
- 1 teaspoon olive oil
- 1 medium onion, chopped
- 1 medium green bell pepper, chopped
- 1 medium rib of celery, thinly sliced
- 1 14.5-ounce can no-salt-added diced tomatoes, undrained
- 1 cup frozen sliced okra
- 1 teaspoon seafood seasoning blend
- ½ teaspoon dried thyme, crumbled
- 2 bay leaves
- 1½ cups water
- ¼ teaspoon salt
- 6 to 8 drops red hot-pepper sauce, or to taste
- 1 cup uncooked instant brown or instant white rice

Heat a large saucepan over medium-high heat. Cook the flour for 1½ to 2 minutes, or until beginning to turn light golden, stirring constantly. Do not overcook. Transfer to a small plate.

In the same saucepan, heat the oil, swirling to coat the bottom. Cook the onion, bell pepper, and celery for 5 minutes, stirring frequently. Stir in the undrained tomatoes, okra, seasoning blend, thyme, and bay leaves. Stir in the flour until well blended. Stir in the water. Increase the heat to high and bring to a boil. Reduce the heat and simmer, covered, for 25 minutes, or until the okra is very tender and the mixture has thickened, stirring frequently. Remove from the heat.

Stir in the salt and hot-pepper sauce. Let stand, covered, for 15 minutes so the flavors blend. Discard the bay leaves.

Meanwhile, prepare the rice using the package directions, omitting the salt and margarine.

To serve, spoon the rice into bowls. Ladle the gumbo over the rice.

Per Serving: Calories 161, Total Fat 2.0 g, Saturated Fat 0.0 g, Polyunsaturated Fat 0.5 g, Monounsaturated Fat 1.0 g, Cholesterol 0 mg, Sodium 355 mg, Carbohydrates 32 g, Dietary Fiber 5 g, Sugars 7 g, Protein 5 g

Dietary Exchanges: 1½ Starch, 2 Vegetable

HEARTY RED BEANS AND RICE

SERVES 4 ▇ *1½ cups per serving*

- 1 cup uncooked instant brown rice or ¾ cup uncooked brown or white basmati rice
- 2 teaspoons olive oil
- 1 medium onion, thinly sliced
- 1 medium red bell pepper, thinly sliced
- 2 medium ribs of celery, diced
- 1 medium eggplant (about 8 ounces), diced
- 2 medium garlic cloves, minced
- 1 15-ounce can no-salt-added red beans, undrained
- 1½ cups low-sodium vegetable broth
- 2 tablespoons imitation bacon bits
- ½ teaspoon salt
- ¼ teaspoon crushed red pepper flakes

Prepare the rice using the package directions, omitting the salt and margarine.

Heat the oil in a large nonstick skillet over medium heat, swirling to coat the bottom. Cook the onion, bell pepper, and celery for 2 to 3 minutes, or until tender-crisp, stirring occasionally. Stir in the eggplant and garlic. Cook for 4 to 5 minutes, or until the eggplant is tender. Add water, 1 tablespoon at a time, if the eggplant sticks to the pan. Stir in the remaining ingredients. Increase the heat to medium high and bring to a simmer. Reduce the heat and simmer, covered, for 10 to 15 minutes, or until the flavors blend, stirring occasionally.

Per Serving: Calories 244, Total Fat 4.0 g, Saturated Fat 0.5 g, Polyunsaturated Fat 0.5 g, Monounsaturated Fat 2.0 g, Cholesterol 0 mg, Sodium 393 mg, Carbohydrates 42 g, Dietary Fiber 9 g, Sugars 6 g, Protein 10 g

Dietary Exchanges: 2 Starch, 3 Vegetable, ½ Fat

CURRIED VEGETABLE CASSEROLE

SERVES 4 ▮ *1½ cups per serving*

    Vegetable oil spray
2   teaspoons olive oil
½   medium red bell pepper, thinly sliced
½   medium onion, thinly sliced
1   small yellow summer squash, thinly sliced
1   small zucchini, thinly sliced
½   cup frozen corn, thawed
½   cup frozen peas, thawed
1   10¾-ounce can reduced-fat, reduced-sodium cream of celery soup
1   cup fat-free half-and-half
1   cup low-sodium vegetable broth
1   teaspoon curry powder
¼   teaspoon salt
¼   teaspoon pepper
1   cup uncooked instant brown rice

Preheat the oven to 375°F. Lightly spray a 13×9×2-inch metal baking pan with vegetable oil spray. (If using glass, reduce the heat to 350°F.)

Heat the oil in a large skillet over medium heat, swirling to coat the bottom. Cook the bell pepper and onion for 2 to 3 minutes, or until tender-crisp, stirring occasionally. Stir in the yellow summer squash and zucchini. Cook for 4 to 5 minutes, or until the vegetables are tender, stirring occasionally. Stir in the corn and peas. Remove from the heat.

Meanwhile, in a large bowl, whisk together the remaining ingredients except the rice.

Stir the vegetable mixture and rice into the soup mixture, combining thoroughly. Spoon into the baking pan. Bake, covered, for 40 to 45 minutes, or until the rice is tender.

Per Serving: Calories 249, Total Fat 4.5 g, Saturated Fat 1.0 g, Polyunsaturated Fat 0.5 g, Monounsaturated Fat 2.0 g, Cholesterol 3 mg, Sodium 517 mg, Carbohydrates 45 g, Dietary Fiber 4 g, Sugars 11 g, Protein 10 g

Dietary Exchanges: 3½ Starch, 1 Vegetable, ½ Fat

TALES FROM THE SOUL
YOLANDA KING

After her mother, Coretta Scott King, suffered a stroke in 2005, Yolanda King teamed up with the American Stroke Association to raise awareness of the risk factors for stroke, especially for African Americans. Following her mother's death in January 2006, Yolanda spoke of her mother's courage in the face of difficulties: "All of her life she was extremely determined to overcome obstacles," Ms. King remembered. "She illustrated that same tenacity after her stroke. It served her well. She was extremely motivated. We saw no depression, though there was some sadness."

Although Ms. King was a young girl when her father, Dr. Martin Luther King, Jr., was assassinated, she emphasizes the role he played in building her character and the importance of continuing both of her parents' legacies to help shape the character of our country. "It's an incredible privilege, a blessing, and a tremendous responsibility," Ms. King says. "To whom much is given, much is required."

> *"Stroke is a health battle that we must take seriously and confront together."*

Ms. King has stepped up to accept that responsibility. She has become the first national spokesperson for the American Stroke Association's Power To End Stroke movement, designed to help educate African Americans about their risk of stroke and methods of prevention. "Since my mother suffered a stroke, I know that it is doubly important for my family and me to pay attention to the risk factors that we can control or eliminate," she says. "That's why we are taking the American Stroke Association's pledge *[see page 25]* and getting serious about reducing our stroke risks for ourselves and our legacy.

"We want African Americans to first take the association's stroke pledge. It's a promise for people to sign, committing not just to survive, but to thrive by doing their part to make the right health choices for themselves, their families, and their communities to prevent and overcome stroke."

Through her involvement with the American Stroke Association, Ms. King knows all too well that someone suffers a stroke every 45 seconds and that stroke is the No. 3 killer in the United States and a leading cause of disability. Having confronted stroke within her own family, Ms. King also puts a face on the fact that the burden of stroke is greater among African Americans than any other ethnic group in America. In fact, blacks are almost twice as likely to have a stroke as whites.

Like many other African Americans, Ms. King was surprised to learn the impact of stroke among blacks. "I was not aware of the huge numbers [of stroke victims] within the African American community, or the fact that we are disproportionately affected," she says. "The situation with my mother has definitely caused me to look at my risk factors, because I fear some of the same issues my mother had. I'm very much at risk."

Although 100,000 African Americans suffer a stroke each year, stroke is, in most cases, not inevitable. Factors such as family history, age, ethnicity, and having had a previous stroke can't be controlled, but others—high blood pressure, smoking, diabetes, obesity, or high cholesterol—can be changed or treated.

"African Americans take on many battles that are often societal challenges," Ms. King says. "Stroke is a health battle that we must take seriously and confront together, because the ramifications can be overwhelming and deadly for you and your loved ones.

"Through Power To End Stroke, we are creating a movement to help each other live stronger, healthier lives. As a people, we must join together to embrace this campaign. The idea of Power To End Stroke is that by simply being aware, people will begin to focus in a way that they haven't before. And that is the necessary first step."

It's never too late to take action against stroke.

Vegetables & Sides

GREEN BEANS AND RED POTATOES

SERVES 6 ▮ *½ cup per serving*

- 8 ounces green beans, trimmed and cut into 2-inch pieces
- 8 ounces red potatoes, cut into ½-inch cubes
- 2 tablespoons snipped fresh parsley
- 1 tablespoon plus 1½ teaspoons light tub margarine
- ¼ teaspoon salt
- ⅛ teaspoon pepper, or to taste
- ⅛ teaspoon paprika

In a large saucepan, steam the green beans and potatoes for 8 minutes, or until the potatoes are tender. Transfer to a medium serving bowl. Add the remaining ingredients. Stir until the paprika is distributed.

Per Serving: Calories 50, Total Fat 1.0 g, Saturated Fat 0.0 g, Polyunsaturated Fat 0.5 g, Monounsaturated Fat 0.5 g, Cholesterol 0 mg, Sodium 125 mg, Carbohydrates 9 g, Dietary Fiber 2 g, Sugars 1 g, Protein 2 g

Dietary Exchanges: ½ Starch

BROCCOLI CHEESE CASSEROLE

SERVES 8 ▪ *½ cup per serving*

> **Vegetable oil spray**
> 1 **pound fresh broccoli florets**
> ½ **cup water**
> 1 **2-ounce jar pimientos, drained**
> ½ **cup fat-free milk**
> ½ **cup fat-free, low-sodium chicken broth**
> 1 **tablespoon plus 1½ teaspoons all-purpose flour**
> ½ **teaspoon onion powder**
> ¼ **teaspoon salt**
> ¼ **teaspoon pepper**
> ⅛ **teaspoon cayenne**
> ½ **cup shredded reduced-fat Cheddar cheese**
> 2 **tablespoons shredded or grated Parmesan cheese**
> 2 **tablespoons chopped walnuts**
> ¼ **cup plain dry bread crumbs**

Preheat the oven to 350°F. Lightly spray a shallow 1½-quart casserole dish with vegetable oil spray.

In a medium saucepan, bring the broccoli and water to a boil over medium-high heat. Reduce the heat and simmer, covered, for 2 minutes, or until the broccoli is tender-crisp. Using a slotted spoon, transfer the broccoli to the casserole dish. Discard the water. Stir the pimientos into the broccoli.

In a small bowl, whisk together the milk, broth, flour, onion powder, salt, pepper, and cayenne until blended (a few lumps of flour may remain). Pour into the same saucepan. Bring to a simmer over medium-high heat, whisking constantly. Cook for 1 to 2 minutes, or until thickened, whisking constantly. Remove from the heat.

Add the Cheddar and Parmesan, whisking for 30 seconds, or until melted. Pour over the broccoli. Sprinkle with the walnuts, then the bread crumbs.

Bake for 20 to 25 minutes, or until the mixture is warmed through and the topping is golden brown.

Per Serving: Calories 80, Total Fat 3.0 g, Saturated Fat 1.5 g, Polyunsaturated Fat 1.0 g, Monounsaturated Fat 0.5 g, Cholesterol 5 mg, Sodium 190 mg, Carbohydrates 8 g, Dietary Fiber 2 g, Sugars 1 g, Protein 6 g

Dietary Exchanges: 1½ Vegetable, ½ Very Lean Meat, ½ Fat

TROPICAL SWEET POTATOES

SERVES 4 ▉ *½ cup per serving*

- 1½ pounds sweet potatoes
-      Vegetable oil spray
- 1   tablespoon firmly packed light brown sugar
- 1½   teaspoons light tub margarine
- ⅛   teaspoon ground nutmeg or ground allspice
-      Scant ⅛ teaspoon rum extract
-      Scant ⅛ teaspoon coconut extract
- 2   teaspoons sweetened flaked coconut (optional)

Put the sweet potatoes in a stockpot. Pour in enough cold water to cover them by 2 inches. Bring to a boil over high heat. Reduce the heat and simmer for 30 to 40 minutes, or until a sharp knife can be easily inserted into a potato. Drain well. Set aside until cool enough to handle.

Preheat the oven to 375°F. Lightly spray a 1-quart casserole dish or 4 ramekins or glass custard cups with vegetable oil spray.

Peel the cooled potatoes and put them in a large mixing bowl. Mash with a potato masher or beat until smooth with an electric mixer. Stir in the remaining ingredients except the coconut. Spoon into the casserole dish, ramekins, or custard cups. Sprinkle with the coconut. Bake for 20 minutes, or until heated through.

Per Serving: Calories 165, Total Fat 0.5 g, Saturated Fat 0.0 g, Polyunsaturated Fat 0.0 g, Monounsaturated Fat 0.5 g, Cholesterol 0 mg, Sodium 106 mg, Carbohydrates 38 g, Dietary Fiber 5 g, Sugars 11 g, Protein 3 g

Dietary Exchanges: 2½ Starch

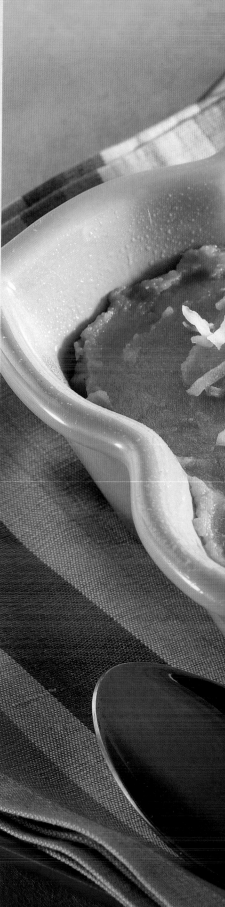

THREE-CHEESE MACARONI BAKE

SERVES 6 ▇ *½ cup per serving*

    Vegetable oil spray
4 **ounces dried elbow macaroni**
½ **cup grated reduced-fat mild Cheddar cheese**
½ **cup fat-free or part-skim ricotta cheese**
⅓ **cup fat-free or light sour cream**
¼ **cup fat-free milk**
    White of 1 large egg
2 **tablespoons grated onion**
1 **tablespoon shredded or grated Parmesan cheese**
1 **teaspoon Worcestershire sauce (lowest sodium available)**
½ **teaspoon no-salt-added all-purpose seasoning blend**
1 **medium Italian plum tomato, cut into 6 slices**
1 **tablespoon plain dry bread crumbs**
1 **teaspoon shredded or grated Parmesan cheese**
¼ **teaspoon garlic powder**

Preheat the oven to 375°F. Lightly spray a 1-quart baking dish or 9×5×3-inch glass or ceramic loaf pan with vegetable oil spray.

In a medium saucepan, prepare the pasta using the package directions, omitting the salt and oil. Place in a colander and drain well.

Meanwhile, in a medium bowl, stir together the Cheddar, ricotta, sour cream, milk, egg white, onion, 1 tablespoon Parmesan, Worcestershire sauce, and seasoning blend. Stir in the pasta. Spoon into the baking dish. Arrange the tomato slices on top.

In a small bowl, stir together the bread crumbs, 1 teaspoon Parmesan, and garlic powder. Sprinkle over the casserole. Lightly spray with vegetable oil spray.

Bake for 30 to 35 minutes, or until heated through and golden brown around the edges.

Per Serving: Calories 134, Total Fat 1.5 g, Saturated Fat 0.5 g, Polyunsaturated Fat 0.0 g, Monounsaturated Fat 0.5 g, Cholesterol 7 mg, Sodium 152 mg, Carbohydrates 20 g, Dietary Fiber 1 g, Sugars 3 g, Protein 10 g

Dietary Exchanges: 1½ Starch, 1 Very Lean Meat

CORNBREAD DRESSING

SERVES 8 ▇ *½ cup per serving*

	Vegetable oil spray
1	**teaspoon olive oil**
4	**medium green onions, thinly sliced**
1	**small rib of celery**
1	**small carrot, chopped**
1½	**cups fat-free, low-sodium chicken broth**
1	**teaspoon dried sage**
¼	**teaspoon pepper**
4	**cups crumbled cornbread**
½	**cup egg substitute**
¼	**cup chopped pecans**

Preheat the oven to 350°F. Lightly spray an 8-inch square baking pan with vegetable oil spray.

In a large skillet, heat the oil over medium heat, swirling to coat the bottom. Cook the green onions, celery, and carrot for 4 to 5 minutes, or until tender, stirring occasionally. Stir in the broth, sage, and pepper.

Put the cornbread in a large bowl. Stir in the vegetable mixture, egg substitute, and pecans (the mixture will be moist). Transfer to the baking pan.

Bake for 30 minutes, or until cooked through and golden brown on top. Transfer to a serving bowl.

Per Serving: Calories 182, Total Fat 7.5 g, Saturated Fat 1.5 g, Polyunsaturated Fat 1.5 g, Monounsaturated Fat 4.0 g, Cholesterol 19 mg, Sodium 364 mg, Carbohydrates 23 g, Dietary Fiber 3 g, Sugars 4 g, Protein 6 g

Dietary Exchanges: 1½ Starch, 1 Fat

Tip *For quick and easy cornbread for this recipe, select a cornbread mix with the lowest amounts of saturated fat, trans fat, and sodium available. Prepare using the package directions, substituting fat-free milk for whole milk and egg substitute for the egg. Omit any butter, margarine, oil, sugar, or salt called for. Bake according to the package directions. Let cool. Crumble 4 cups of the cornbread with your fingers and use as directed in the dressing recipe.*

MIXED GREENS AND CABBAGE

SERVES 8 ▮ *about ½ cup per serving*

- 1 teaspoon olive oil
- ½ medium onion, thinly sliced
- 2 cups fat-free, low-sodium chicken broth
- 2 tablespoons imitation bacon bits
- 1 teaspoon garlic powder
- 1 teaspoon celery seeds
- ¼ teaspoon pepper
- ¼ teaspoon crushed red pepper flakes
- 4 ounces fresh collard greens
- 4 ounces fresh kale
- 8 ounces green cabbage

In a large saucepan, heat the oil over medium heat, swirling to coat the bottom. Cook the onion for 2 to 3 minutes, or until tender-crisp, stirring occasionally.

Stir in the broth, bacon bits, garlic powder, celery seeds, pepper, and red pepper flakes. Increase the heat to medium high and bring to a simmer. Reduce the heat and continue to simmer, covered, for 4 to 5 minutes so the flavors blend.

Meanwhile, trim the stems from the collard greens and kale. Discard the stems. Core the cabbage. Discard the core. Coarsely chop the greens and cabbage. Stir into the broth mixture. Increase the heat to medium high and bring to a simmer. Reduce the heat and simmer, covered, for 35 to 45 minutes, or until the greens and cabbage are tender, stirring occasionally. Ladle the greens and pot likker (cooking liquid) into bowls.

Per Serving: Calories 36, Total Fat 1.0 g, Saturated Fat 0.0 g, Polyunsaturated Fat 0.0 g, Monounsaturated Fat 0.5 g, Cholesterol 0 mg, Sodium 61 mg, Carbohydrates 5 g, Dietary Fiber 2 g, Sugars 2 g, Protein 2 g

Dietary Exchanges: 1 Vegetable

SLOW-COOKER PINTO BEANS

SERVES 12 ■ *½ cup per serving*

    8 **ounces dried pinto beans (about 1¼ cups)**

    3 **cups fat-free, low-sodium chicken broth**

    1 **small carrot, chopped**

   ½ **medium rib of celery, chopped**

   ¼ **medium onion, chopped**

    2 **ounces reduced-fat smoked sausage (lowest fat and sodium available), diced**

    2 **tablespoons imitation bacon bits**

    1 **medium jalapeño pepper, ribs and seeds discarded, diced (use plastic gloves while handling)**

   ½ **teaspoon salt**

   ¼ **teaspoon pepper**

Sort through the beans, removing any shriveled beans or stones. Put the beans in a large bowl and cover with cold water by 2 inches. Let soak for 3 to 12 hours. Drain in a colander. Transfer to a slow cooker.

Stir in the remaining ingredients. Cook, covered, on high for 4 to 5 hours or on low for 8 to 10 hours, or until the beans and vegetables are tender. If the mixture gets too dry, add water ½ cup at a time. (If your cooker does not have a glass lid, check after about 2 hours if cooking on high, or about 4 hours if cooking on low. Continue checking about every 30 minutes.) Ladle the beans and pot likker (cooking liquid) into bowls.

Per Serving: Calories 81, Total Fat 1.0 g, Saturated Fat 0.0 g, Polyunsaturated Fat 0.0 g, Monounsaturated Fat 0.5 g, Cholesterol 3 mg, Sodium 175 mg, Carbohydrates 13 g, Dietary Fiber 4 g, Sugars 1 g, Protein 6 g

Dietary Exchanges: 1 Starch, ½ Very Lean Meat

TIME-SAVER *Substitute three 15-ounce cans no-salt-added pinto beans with their liquid for the dried beans. Pour into a large saucepan. Add the remaining ingredients, reducing the broth to 1½ cups. Bring to a simmer over medium-high heat, stirring occasionally. Reduce the heat and simmer, covered, for 15 to 20 minutes, or until the vegetables are tender and the flavors blend.*

SUCCOTASH WITH THYME

SERVES 6 ◼ *½ cup per serving*

- **2 cups water**
- **1 cup frozen baby lima beans or Fordhook lima beans**
- **1 cup frozen cut green beans**
- **½ teaspoon dried thyme, crumbled**
- **2 cups frozen corn kernels**
- **2 tablespoons light tub margarine**
- **¼ teaspoon salt**

In a medium saucepan, bring the water to a boil over high heat. Stir in the lima beans, green beans, and thyme. Return to a boil. Reduce the heat and simmer, covered, for 10 minutes. Stir in the corn. Cook, covered, for 5 minutes, or until the lima beans are tender. Drain well in a colander. Pour into a serving bowl. Stir in the margarine and salt.

Per Serving: Calories 100, Total Fat 2.0 g, Saturated Fat 0.0 g, Polyunsaturated Fat 0.5 g, Monounsaturated Fat 1.0 g, Cholesterol 0 mg, Sodium 197 mg, Carbohydrates 19 g, Dietary Fiber 3 g, Sugars 3 g, Protein 3 g

Dietary Exchanges: 1½ Starch

Tip *Of the two varieties of lima beans—baby limas and Fordhooks, or butter beans—baby limas are smaller and milder tasting.*

OVEN-FRIED OKRA

SERVES 4 ▮ *½ cup per serving*

- **2** teaspoons canola or corn oil
- ¼ cup all-purpose flour
- **1** teaspoon salt-free Cajun or Creole seasoning blend *(see tip on page 78)*
- ¼ teaspoon salt
- ¼ teaspoon pepper
- **8** ounces fresh okra, stems discarded, cut into ½-inch slices, or 2 cups frozen sliced okra, thawed
- ¼ cup egg substitute
- ½ cup yellow cornmeal
- Vegetable oil spray

Preheat the oven to 400°F. Drizzle the oil over a rimmed baking sheet, tilting to coat.

In a medium resealable plastic bag, combine the flour, seasoning blend, salt, and pepper. Add the okra, seal the bag, and shake to coat.

Put the egg substitute and cornmeal in separate shallow bowls. Set the bowl with the egg substitute, the bowl with the cornmeal, and the baking sheet in a row, assembly-line fashion. Using a slotted spoon, transfer about one-fourth of the okra to the egg substitute, stirring to coat. Let any excess liquid drip back into the bowl. Add the coated okra to the cornmeal, stirring to coat. Transfer to the baking sheet, arranging the okra in a single layer and leaving space between the pieces so they will brown evenly. Repeat with batches of the remaining okra. Lightly spray the okra with the vegetable oil spray.

Bake for 20 to 25 minutes, or until the okra is crisp on the outside and tender on the inside when tested with a fork. Transfer to a serving bowl.

Per Serving: Calories 136, Total Fat 3.0 g, Saturated Fat 0.5 g, Polyunsaturated Fat 1.0 g, Monounsaturated Fat 1.5 g, Cholesterol 0 mg, Sodium 182 mg, Carbohydrates 25 g, Dietary Fiber 3 g, Sugars 1 g, Protein 5 g

Dietary Exchanges: 1½ Starch, 1 Vegetable, ½ Fat

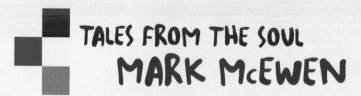

TALES FROM THE SOUL
MARK McEWEN

To a journalist, the ultimate compliment is to be told he has ink in his veins. Mark McEwen is a great example of someone who does. The newsman, best known for his 16 years as the weatherman, entertainment reporter, and anchor for "The Early Show" on CBS, is still writing and reporting despite suffering a near-fatal stroke in November 2005.

> *"I thought I would live forever and that things like stroke happen to other people, not to me."*

McEwen, then 51, was working as an anchor for WKMG-TV in Orlando, Florida. While on the road in Maryland, he felt so poorly he went to a hospital emergency room. "I was told I had the stomach flu," he recalls. "Two days later, after becoming ill on a flight, I was admitted to Sand Lake Hospital in Orlando."

That "stomach flu" was actually a transient ischemic attack (TIA), or mini-stroke, which produces strokelike symptoms but no lasting damage. McEwen subsequently experienced a massive and debilitating stroke caused by a blood clot blocking oxygen to his brain.

For four days, McEwen hovered near death, drifting in and out of consciousness. During a period of lucidity, he recognized family members gathered around his bed and immediately knew that something was terribly wrong. "I still didn't realize what my symptoms meant," he says, "but I knew it must be very bad for my family to fly in from Seattle, Maryland, and Los Angeles."

Against all odds, McEwen survived the stroke. When discharged, he was bedridden, could barely speak, and couldn't use his right hand—all serious obstacles for a journalist known for his smooth and fluent on-air manner. McEwen remembers thinking, "My life will be completely different now, and I will be starting over.

"Where the clot lodged in my brain affected my balance, fine motor skills, and speaking," he says. "Hey, that's pretty much my whole job right there."

Ever the journalist, the first thing he did after his release was to learn everything he could about stroke. He also began to set goals, such as moving from a bed to a wheelchair, then from a wheelchair to a walker. He worked daily to regain use of his right hand, his balance, and, most importantly, his voice.

Today, McEwen still has a way to go, but he's speaking more clearly, walking and driving, and seeing to his personal needs. And he's writing a book, "Change in the Weather: Life After Stroke." Soon he'll be back on the air, starting with a public service announcement and some hour-long specials. He remains optimistic that he'll resume his duties at the anchor desk.

McEwen had no family history of stroke and did not smoke. However, he was being treated for high blood pressure and was working in a notoriously high-pressure job. He worked out sporadically, was a little on the heavy side, and wasn't all that careful about his diet.

He didn't know that African Americans have almost twice the risk of first-ever stroke compared with whites. "Before my stroke, I thought I would live forever and that things like stroke happen to other people, not to me," he says. McEwen's prestroke attitude reflects that of many other African Americans, according to a new American Heart Association survey, which finds that 72% of African Americans don't believe they will ever have a stroke.

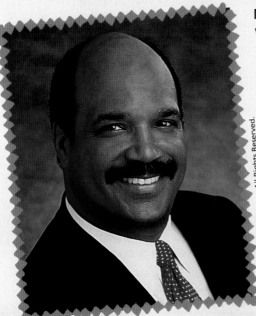

© 2001 CBS Broadcasting Inc. All Rights Reserved.

McEwen now watches his weight, works out regularly, and eats more fish, whole grains, fruits, and vegetables. "I sure don't eat salt and sugar like I used to," he says. As part of his ongoing rehabilitation, McEwen undergoes hyperbaric treatments to saturate his brain with oxygen and promote healing, undergoes acupuncture, and reads aloud several newspapers each day as speech therapy. He credits his wife, Denise, with much of his remarkable progress. The McEwens and their four children—Maya, 11; Jenna, 10; and identical twins Miles and Griffin, 3—make their home in central Florida.

The newsman's fan base doesn't end with his family, though. Legendary singer Tony Bennett, whom McEwen once interviewed, is now a friend who calls regularly with words of encouragement. McEwen says, "Tony tells me that I am the first person he has ever heard of who has come back from a stroke."

Breads & Breakfasts

SWEET POTATO MUFFINS

SERVES 24 ■ *1 muffin per serving*

Vegetable oil spray (optional)
1 18.5-ounce package spice cake mix
1 13-ounce can sweet potatoes packed with no liquid or in light syrup, drained if needed
½ cup uncooked quick-cooking oatmeal
½ cup egg substitute
½ cup water
2 teaspoons grated orange zest
½ cup fresh orange juice
1 tablespoon ground cinnamon

Preheat the oven to 350°F. Lightly spray two 12-cup muffin pans with vegetable oil spray or put paper muffin cups in the pans.

In a large mixing bowl, stir all the ingredients together. Using an electric mixer, beat according to the package directions. Spoon the batter into the muffin cups.

Bake for 22 to 24 minutes, or until a cake tester or wooden tooth-pick inserted in the center of a muffin in the middle of the pan comes out clean. Transfer the muffins from the pans to a cooling rack. Let cool for 15 to 20 minutes before serving.

Per Serving: Calories 115, Total Fat 1.5 g, Saturated Fat 1.0 g, Polyunsaturated Fat 0.0 g, Monounsaturated Fat 0.5 g, Cholesterol 0 mg, Sodium 159 mg, Carbohydrates 24 g, Dietary Fiber 1 g, Sugars 12 g, Protein 2 g

Dietary Exchanges: 1½ Other Carbohydrate, ½ Fat

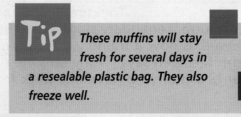

Tip *These muffins will stay fresh for several days in a resealable plastic bag. They also freeze well.*

ZUCCHINI NUT BREAD

SERVES 12 *1 slice per serving*

	Vegetable oil spray
1	**cup all-purpose flour**
½	**cup whole-wheat flour**
½	**cup sugar**
2	**teaspoons ground cinnamon**
1½	**teaspoons baking powder**
½	**teaspoon baking soda**
⅛	**teaspoon salt**
⅛	**teaspoon ground nutmeg**
1	**cup finely grated zucchini (about 6 ounces)**
¼	**cup chopped pecans, dry-roasted**
½	**cup fat-free or light sour cream**
¼	**cup unsweetened applesauce**
1	**large egg, or ¼ cup egg substitute plus 1 teaspoon canola or corn oil**
	White of 1 large egg
2	**to 3 teaspoons grated lemon zest**
1	**teaspoon vanilla extract**

Preheat the oven to 350°F. Lightly spray a 9×5×3-inch loaf pan with vegetable oil spray.

In a medium bowl, stir together the flours, sugar, cinnamon, baking powder, baking soda, salt, and nutmeg. Add the zucchini and pecans, stirring to coat.

In another medium bowl, whisk together the remaining ingredients. Add to the flour mixture, stirring until just combined. Do not overmix; the batter should be slightly lumpy. Pour the batter into the loaf pan, smoothing the top.

Bake for 50 to 55 minutes, or until a cake tester or wooden toothpick inserted in the center comes out clean. Let cool in the pan for 5 minutes. Turn out onto a cooling rack and let cool completely before slicing.

Per Serving: Calories 128, Total Fat 2.5 g, Saturated Fat 0.5 g, Polyunsaturated Fat 0.5 g, Monounsaturated Fat 1.0 g, Cholesterol 19 mg, Sodium 147 mg, Carbohydrates 23 g, Dietary Fiber 2 g, Sugars 10 g, Protein 4 g

Dietary Exchanges: 1½ Starch

Tip
To dry-roast nuts, put them in a single layer in an ungreased skillet. Cook over medium heat for about 4 minutes, or until just fragrant, stirring frequently.

SKILLET HAM HASH

SERVES 4 ▪ *1 cup per serving*

- 2 teaspoons olive oil
- 1 large green bell pepper, diced
- 1 large red bell pepper, diced
- 1 medium onion, diced
- ½ cup diced lower-sodium, low-fat ham (about 4 ounces), all visible fat discarded
- 3 cups frozen fat-free southern-style diced hash brown potatoes, thawed
- ½ teaspoon salt-free Cajun or Creole seasoning blend
- 2 tablespoons snipped fresh parsley
- ¼ teaspoon salt
- ¼ teaspoon pepper

In a large nonstick skillet, heat the oil over medium heat, swirling to coat the bottom. Cook the bell peppers and onion for 4 to 5 minutes, or until tender, stirring occasionally. Stir in the ham. Cook for 1 to 2 minutes, or until warmed through, stirring occasionally.

Stir in the hash browns and seasoning blend. Cook without stirring for 4 minutes, or until the bottom is golden brown. Stir (the golden-brown pieces will be redistributed). Cook without stirring for 4 minutes, or until the bottom is golden brown and the mixture is warmed through.

Stir in the parsley, salt, and pepper. Spoon onto plates.

Tip *If you can't find salt-free Cajun or Creole seasoning blend or just prefer to make your own, stir together 1 teaspoon each chile powder, onion powder, garlic powder, dried thyme, paprika, and ground cumin in a small bowl. Makes 2 tablespoons. Store in an airtight container for up to 6 months.*

Per Serving: Calories 207, Total Fat 3.5 g, Saturated Fat 0.5 g, Polyunsaturated Fat 0.5 g, Monounsaturated Fat 2.0 g, Cholesterol 12 mg, Sodium 420 mg, Carbohydrates 37 g, Dietary Fiber 5 g, Sugars 6 g, Protein 9 g

Dietary Exchanges: 2 Starch, 1½ Vegetable, ½ Lean Meat

TURKEY SAUSAGE AND GRITS BREAKFAST CASSEROLE

SERVES 4 ■ *1 cup per serving*

      Vegetable oil spray
1¼ **cups fat-free, low-sodium chicken broth**
 1 **cup fat-free milk**
⅛ **teaspoon cayenne**
½ **cup uncooked quick-cooking grits**
 2 **tablespoons shredded or grated Parmesan cheese**
 2 **cups egg substitute**
½ **cup diced cooked turkey sausage patties (about 3 ounces)**

Preheat the oven to 350°F. Lightly spray an 8-inch square baking pan with vegetable oil spray.

In a medium saucepan, whisk together the broth, milk, and cayenne. Bring to a simmer over medium-high heat. Gradually add the grits, whisking constantly. Reduce the heat and simmer for 5 minutes, or until thickened, whisking occasionally. Whisk in the Parmesan. Remove from the heat. Let cool for about 5 minutes.

While the grits cool, heat a large nonstick skillet over medium heat. Cook the egg substitute and turkey sausage for 3 to 5 minutes, stirring as needed to scramble the eggs. Stir the mixture into the grits. Pour into the baking pan.

Bake for 20 minutes, or until the casserole is warmed through.

Per Serving: Calories 174, Total Fat 4.0 g, Saturated Fat 1.5 g, Polyunsaturated Fat 0.5 g, Monounsaturated Fat 0.5 g, Cholesterol 23 mg, Sodium 406 mg, Carbohydrates 14 g, Dietary Fiber 1 g, Sugars 5 g, Protein 20 g

Dietary Exchanges: 1 Starch, 2½ Very Lean Meat

SAVORY SPOON BREAD

SERVES 12 ▮ *¼ cup per serving*

> **Vegetable oil spray**
> 1 **cup fat-free milk**
> 1 **cup fat-free half-and-half**
> 2 **medium green onions, thinly sliced**
> 1 **tablespoon imitation bacon bits**
> ½ **teaspoon salt**
> ⅛ **teaspoon cayenne**
> 1 **cup white cornmeal**
> **Whites of 4 large eggs**
> ½ **cup egg substitute**
> 2 **tablespoons light tub margarine**

Preheat the oven to 375°F. Lightly spray a 2-quart soufflé dish or casserole dish with vegetable oil spray.

In a medium saucepan, whisk together the milk, half-and-half, green onions, bacon bits, salt, and cayenne. Bring to a simmer over medium-high heat. Gradually add the cornmeal, whisking constantly. Cook for 1 minute, or until thickened. Remove from the heat. Let cool for about 5 minutes.

Meanwhile, in a medium mixing bowl, beat the egg whites with an electric mixer on medium high for 2 to 3 minutes, or until stiff peaks form (do not beat until dry).

Stir the egg substitute and margarine into the cornmeal mixture. Using a rubber scraper, fold gently into the egg whites until the whites are incorporated. (It is okay for a few streaks of the whites to be visible; try to keep from deflating the whites by overmixing.) Pour into the baking dish.

Bake for 35 to 40 minutes, or until the crust is golden brown and when a spoonful is removed from the center, it is warm to the touch and looks creamy. If you prefer to test with an instant-read thermometer, the internal temperature should be at least 160°F.

Per Serving: Calories 83, Total Fat 1.0 g, Saturated Fat 0.0 g, Polyunsaturated Fat 0.5 g, Monounsaturated Fat 0.5 g, Cholesterol 0 mg, Sodium 188 mg, Carbohydrates 14 g, Dietary Fiber 1 g, Sugars 3 g, Protein 5 g
Dietary Exchanges: 1 Starch

Desserts

ORANGE POUND CAKE WITH MIXED BERRIES

SERVES 16 ▮ *2 (½-inch) slices cake and scant 3 tablespoons berry mixture per serving*

Cake

- 1 16-ounce pound cake mix
- ¾ cup fat-free milk
  Whites of 4 large eggs or ½ cup egg substitute
- ¼ cup all-fruit apricot spread
- 1 tablespoon plus 1 teaspoon grated orange zest

Topping

- 16 ounces frozen mixed berries
- ¼ cup fresh orange juice
- ½ cup all-fruit apricot fruit spread

Preheat the oven to 350°F.

In a medium mixing bowl, stir together the cake ingredients. Using an electric mixer, beat according to the package directions. Pour the batter into 2 nonstick 8½×4½×2½-inch loaf pans, smoothing the tops.

Bake for 27 minutes, or until a cake tester or wooden toothpick inserted in the center comes out almost clean. Transfer the pans to cooling racks. Let cool for 10 minutes. Invert the cake onto the racks and let cool completely, about 1 hour.

Meanwhile, in a medium bowl, stir together the frozen berries and orange juice.

In a small microwaveable bowl, microwave the ½ cup fruit spread on 100 percent power (high) for 20 seconds, or until melted. Gently stir

into the berry mixture. Cover with plastic wrap. Let stand for 1 hour so the berries thaw and the flavors blend. Refrigerate until serving time.

To serve, cut the cake into ½-inch slices. Transfer to dessert plates. Top each serving with the berry mixture.

Per Serving: Calories 182, Total Fat 4.5 g, Saturated Fat 1.0 g, Polyunsaturated Fat 0.0 g, Monounsaturated Fat 0.0 g, Cholesterol 0 mg, Sodium 170 mg, Carbohydrates 33 g, Dietary Fiber 1 g, Sugars 20 g, Protein 3 g

Dietary Exchanges: 2 Other Carbohydrate, 1 Fat

RED VELVET SHEET CAKE

SERVES 36 ■ *one 2½×2-inch piece per serving*

Vegetable oil spray
1 **18.25-ounce yellow cake mix**
1 **cup water**
2 **tablespoons unsweetened cocoa powder**
½ **cup unsweetened applesauce**
⅓ **cup low-fat buttermilk**
¾ **cup egg substitute**
1 **tablespoon red food coloring**
4 **ounces fat-free or reduced-fat cream cheese, softened**
2 **cups confectioners' sugar, sifted**
1 **tablespoon fat-free milk**
1 **teaspoon vanilla extract**
1½ **to 3 teaspoons fat-free milk (optional)**
2 **or 3 drops red food coloring**

Preheat the oven to 350°F. Lightly spray an 18×13×1-inch rimmed baking sheet with vegetable oil spray.

Prepare the cake mix using the package directions but substituting the water and cocoa powder for the amount of water called for in the directions, the applesauce and buttermilk for the oil, and the egg substitute for the eggs. Stir in 1 tablespoon red food coloring. Pour the batter into the baking sheet.

Bake for 18 to 20 minutes, or until a cake tester or wooden toothpick inserted in the center comes out clean. Transfer the cake in the pan to a cooling rack. Let cool completely, at least 1 hour.

In a medium mixing bowl, beat the cream cheese with an electric mixer on medium until smooth. Add the confectioners' sugar, 1 tablespoon milk, and vanilla, stirring gently until most of the sugar has been blended in. Beat on medium until smooth. The icing should spread easily. If it is too thick, gradually stir in the remaining milk until the desired consistency.

Transfer 2 tablespoons icing to a small bowl. Add the remaining food coloring, stirring until a uniform pink.

Spoon the white icing onto the center of the cake. Using a rubber scraper, spread the icing evenly over the cake, leaving a ½-inch

margin around the edges. Decoratively drizzle the pink icing over the white icing, still leaving the cake un-iced around the edges.

Per Serving: Calories 93, Total Fat 1.0 g, Saturated Fat 0.5 g, Polyunsaturated Fat 0.0 g, Monounsaturated Fat 0.5 g, Cholesterol 1 mg, Sodium 128 mg, Carbohydrates 20 g, Dietary Fiber 0 g, Sugars 14 g, Protein 1 g

Dietary Exchanges: 1½ Other Carbohydrate, ½ Fat

WARM PEACH BREAD PUDDING

SERVES 4 ▮ *1 ramekin per serving*

Vegetable oil spray

4 slices day-old reduced-calorie bread (whole-wheat or multigrain preferred), crust discarded, bread diced into ½-inch cubes (about 2 cups)

⅔ cup fresh or frozen peaches, partially thawed, or fresh apple, such as McIntosh, Jonagold, or Golden Delicious, peeled, cut into bite-size pieces

Whites of 2 large eggs, or 1 large egg

2 to 3 tablespoons firmly packed light brown sugar

12 ounces fat-free evaporated milk

½ ounce maple syrup

¼ ounce dark rum, light rum, or bourbon

½ teaspoon vanilla extract

¼ teaspoon ground cinnamon

¼ teaspoon ground nutmeg

⅛ teaspoon salt

⅛ teaspoon ground ginger (optional)

6 cups water

¼ cup (about) fresh fruit or ¼ cup fat-free or light frozen whipped topping, thawed, for garnish (optional)

Preheat the oven to 325°F. Lightly spray four 5-ounce porcelain ramekins or glass custard cups with vegetable oil spray.

In a medium bowl, stir together the bread cubes and fruit. Spoon into the ramekins.

In a small bowl, gently whisk together the egg whites and brown sugar until well blended. Gently whisk in the evaporated milk, maple syrup, rum, vanilla, cinnamon, nutmeg, salt, and ginger. Pour as much of the mixture as possible into the ramekins, making sure the bread cubes are soaked. Refrigerate for 10 minutes so the bread cubes will absorb the liquid.

Meanwhile, pour the water into a medium saucepan and bring to a boil over high heat.

Arrange the ramekins in a large rectangular pan, such as a 13×9×2-inch baking dish, so they are evenly spaced, leaving at least 1 inch between ramekins. Place the pan in the oven. Slowly pour the hot water into the pan until about a third of the way up the sides of the

ramekins, being careful to keep the water out of the ramekins.

Bake for about 35 minutes, or until the tip of a knife inserted in the center comes out almost clean and the custard is almost set (it should jiggle slightly in the center when gently shaken). Very carefully remove the ramekins from the water bath and dry them off. Let cool on a cooling rack for 5 minutes. Garnish with fresh fruit or whipped topping.

Per Serving: Calories 189, Total Fat 1.0 g, Saturated Fat 0.0 g, Polyunsaturated Fat 0.5 g, Monounsaturated Fat 0.0 g, Cholesterol 4 mg, Sodium 332 mg, Carbohydrates 35 g, Dietary Fiber 3 g, Sugars 25 g, Protein 11 g

Dietary Exchanges: 1½ Starch, 1 Skim Milk

BANANAS FOSTER RICE PUDDING

SERVES 4 ▌ *½ cup per serving*

- ¾ **cup fat-free half-and-half**
- ½ **cup uncooked quick-cooking brown rice**
- ¼ **cup golden raisins**
- ¼ **cup firmly packed dark or light brown sugar**
- 1 **teaspoon grated orange zest**
- 2 **tablespoons fresh orange juice**
- 1 **tablespoon light tub margarine**
- ½ **teaspoon ground cinnamon**
- ½ **teaspoon rum extract**
- ⅛ **teaspoon ground nutmeg**
- 2 **medium bananas, cut crosswise into ½-inch slices**

In a medium saucepan, bring the half-and-half, rice, and raisins to a simmer over medium-high heat, stirring occasionally. Reduce the heat and simmer, covered, for 10 minutes, or until the rice is tender. Remove the pan from the heat. Cover to keep warm.

Meanwhile, in a medium skillet, stir together the remaining ingredients except the bananas. Cook over medium heat for 3 to 5 minutes, or until the mixture is warmed through and the brown sugar is dissolved, stirring occasionally. Stir in the bananas. Cook for 2 to 3 minutes, or until the bananas are warmed through, stirring occasionally.

Pour the banana mixture into the rice mixture. Stir gently to combine. Spoon into bowls. Serve warm.

Per Serving: Calories 225, Total Fat 2.0 g, Saturated Fat 0.0 g, Polyunsaturated Fat 0.5 g, Monounsaturated Fat 1.0 g, Cholesterol 0 mg, Sodium 77 mg, Carbohydrates 51 g, Dietary Fiber 3 g, Sugars 30 g, Protein 5 g

Dietary Exchanges: 1½ Fruit, 2 Other Carbohydrate, ½ Fat

LEMONADE TEA CAKES

SERVES 20 ▮ *2 cookies per serving*

Vegetable oil spray
- 3 **cups all-purpose flour**
- 1 **teaspoon baking soda**
- 1½ **cups sugar**
- ⅔ **cup light tub margarine**
- ½ **cup egg substitute**
- ⅓ **cup frozen lemonade concentrate, thawed**
- 1 **teaspoon grated lemon zest**
- 1 **teaspoon vanilla extract**
- 3 **tablespoons red decorating sugar**

Preheat the oven to 400°F. Lightly spray 2 baking sheets with vegetable oil spray.

In a medium bowl, whisk together the flour and baking soda.

In a separate medium bowl, with an electric mixer, beat the sugar and margarine on medium speed until well blended. Pour in the egg substitute. Beat until well blended.

In a small bowl, whisk together the lemonade concentrate, lemon zest, and vanilla.

Alternately add the flour mixture and the lemonade mixture to the margarine mixture, beating on low speed after each addition. Do not overmix, or the cookies will be tough. Drop the dough on the cookie sheets in portions of 1½ tablespoons, about 2 inches apart. Sprinkle with the red sugar.

Bake for 8 to 9 minutes, or until golden brown. Transfer the baking sheets to cooling racks. Let the cookies cool on the baking sheets for 2 to 3 minutes. Transfer the cookies onto the cooling racks and let cool completely. Store in airtight containers at room temperature or in the refrigerator, or freeze for up to 2 months.

Per Serving: Calories 168, Total Fat 2.5 g, Saturated Fat 0.0 g, Polyunsaturated Fat 0.5 g, Monounsaturated Fat 1.5 g, Cholesterol 0 mg, Sodium 124 mg, Carbohydrates 34 g, Dietary Fiber 1 g, Sugars 19 g, Protein 3 g

Dietary Exchanges: 2½ Other Carbohydrate, ½ Fat

Get Involved

We invite you to join us in the fight against cardiovascular disease and stroke. Please call **1-800-AHA-USA1 (1-800-242-8721)** or visit **americanheart.org** for information on how you can get involved. For information on stroke, call **1-888-4-STROKE** or visit **StrokeAssociation.org**.

The Heart Of Diabetes: Understanding Insulin ResistanceSM helps people with diabetes take action to reduce their risk for cardiovascular disease. This program helps raise awareness that diabetes dramatically increases a person's risk for heart disease and stroke and often is associated with risk factors such as high blood pressure, cholesterol disorders, obesity, and insulin resistance.

Search Your Heart/Conozca Su Corazón is a community-based education program that targets heart disease and stroke and provides tools to promote heart-healthy lifestyles to African Americans and Hispanics/Latinos.

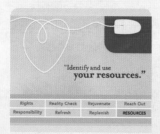

The American Heart Association's newest Web site, **americanheart.org/caregiver**, is dedicated to the 50 million family caregivers in the United States today. Including sections titled "Refresh," "Rejuvenate," "Reach Out," and "Replenish," the site features all the tools and advice you'll need to take care of someone with heart disease—and yourself.

American Heart Association® | American Stroke Association®

Learn and Live℠

CHOOSE TO MOVE ℠

Choose To Move℠ is a free 12-week program that shows women how to love their bodies by exercising regularly, selecting nutritious foods, and taking time for themselves. Becoming more active and eating well will help women better juggle work, family, and life's other demands.

American Heart Association

Learn and Live®

Start! is a national movement that calls on all Americans and their employers to create a culture of encouraging physical activity and good health through walking so people will live longer, heart-healthy lives.

Look to the American Heart Association Food Certification Program for help in food selection. The program's heart-check mark is an easy, reliable tool you can use while grocery shopping to quickly identify products that are heart-healthy. For a complete list of certified products, visit **heartcheckmark.org**. Use the online grocery list builder to create and print a heart-healthy shopping list you can take to the store.

American Heart Association

Meets American Heart Association food criteria for saturated fat and cholesterol for healthy people over age 2.

The **American Heart Association Consumer Publications** include a bestselling library of cookbooks and consumer health books. The *American Heart Association Low-Salt Cookbook, Third Edition,* is the perfect guide to learning how to prepare satisfying and healthy meals that are also low in sodium. With more than 200 mouthwatering recipes, this book proves that a low-salt diet is not only good for you but delicious too.

Look for these other American Heart Association publications wherever books are sold:

American Heart Association No-Fad Diet: A Personal Plan for Healthy Weight Loss

The New American Heart Association Cookbook, Seventh Edition

American Heart Association Low-Fat, Low-Cholesterol Cookbook, Third Edition

American Heart Association Low-Calorie Cookbook

American Heart Association Quick & Easy Cookbook

American Heart Association Meals in Minutes Cookbook

American Heart Association One-Dish Meals

Stroke Connection Magazine provides support to stroke survivors and their families with inspiring stories from fellow survivors and caregivers. It also includes practical tips for daily living, information on reducing the risk of another stroke, and news about stroke treatments, research, public policy, and programs. This four-color magazine is published six times a year and is free to individual subscribers.

To subscribe to *Stroke Connection Magazine* or for more information on stroke-related programs, call the American Stroke Association at **1-888-4-STROKE** or visit **StrokeAssociation.org**.

Recipe Index

Metric Conversion Chart

VOLUME MEASUREMENTS (dry)

1/8 teaspoon = 0.5 mL
1/4 teaspoon = 1 mL
1/2 teaspoon = 2 mL
3/4 teaspoon = 4 mL
1 teaspoon = 5 mL
1 tablespoon = 15 mL
2 tablespoons = 30 mL
1/4 cup = 60 mL
1/3 cup = 75 mL
1/2 cup = 125 mL
2/3 cup = 150 mL
3/4 cup = 175 mL
1 cup = 250 mL
2 cups = 1 pint = 500 mL
3 cups = 750 mL
4 cups = 1 quart = 1 L

VOLUME MEASUREMENTS (fluid)

1 fluid ounce (2 tablespoons) = 30 mL
4 fluid ounces (1/2 cup) = 125 mL
8 fluid ounces (1 cup) = 250 mL
12 fluid ounces (1 1/2 cups) = 375 mL
16 fluid ounces (2 cups) = 500 mL

WEIGHTS (mass)

1/2 ounce = 15 g
1 ounce = 30 g
3 ounces = 90 g
4 ounces = 120 g
8 ounces = 225 g
10 ounces = 285 g
12 ounces = 360 g
16 ounces = 1 pound = 450 g

DIMENSIONS

1/16 inch = 2 mm
1/8 inch = 3 mm
1/4 inch = 6 mm
1/2 inch = 1.5 cm
3/4 inch = 2 cm
1 inch = 2.5 cm

OVEN TEMPERATURES

250°F = 120°C
275°F = 140°C
300°F = 150°C
325°F = 160°C
350°F = 180°C
375°F = 190°C
400°F = 200°C
425°F = 220°C
450°F = 230°C

BAKING PAN SIZES

Utensil	Size in Inches/Quarts	Metric Volume	Size in Centimeters
Baking or	8×8×2	2 L	20×20×5
Cake Pan	9×9×2	2.5 L	23×23×5
(square or	12×8×2	3 L	30×20×5
rectangular)	13×9×2	3.5 L	33×23×5
Loaf Pan	8×4×3	1.5 L	20×10×7
	9×5×3	2 L	23×13×7
Round Layer	8×1½	1.2 L	20×4
Cake Pan	9×1½	1.5 L	23×4
Pie Plate	8×1¼	750 mL	20×3
	9×1¼	1 L	23×3
Baking Dish	1 quart	1 L	—
or Casserole	1½ quarts	1.5 L	—
	2 quarts	2 L	—

Notes

_____

_____

_____

_____

_____

_____

_____

_____

_____

_____

_____

_____

_____

_____

_____

_____